IN TULIP'S TIME

A BULMER CRAFTSMAN'S MEMORIES

Extracts from the writings of

Philip Tulip Rowe

(1871 – 1955)

Vol. I

Edited by Robin Rowe

Published by
Philip Rowe Archive – Bulmer, Essex

Published by
Philip Rowe Archive – Bulmer, Essex

2004

ISBN 0-9548936-0-3

Acknowledgements.

The editor thanks the following for all their help. First of all I am indebted to the initial encouragement given me by Bulmer local historian, the late Basil Slaughter, one winter's night in early 1988. Then to my cousin Peter Rowe for family information and both he and Ashley Cooper for their encouragement, constructive criticism and help with background information and local knowledge. The annotated margins are indeed one of Ashley's bright ideas. Peter's father, the late Tom Rowe, provided family and other background information, and he, together with those relatives who have passed on their copies of the original manuscripts, namely Peter Rowe, the late (aunt) Mary Rowe, and Gordon Rowe, are thanked for their willingness to cooperate. Thanks go to all those who have perused the final draft and added their comment and encouragement, especially Joan Brown, Evelyn Reeve and John Dixey. I am particularly indebted to David Hardwick for his help with the scanning and embellishment of old photographs and line drawings. Nearer home I wish to thank wiz-kid Jess and her aunties for coming to the rescue on numerous occasions when the computer has decided to go its own way, and the long-suffering Freda who has picked up the pieces.

(Prepared and sold in association with The Bulmer Local History Society)

Printed for the publisher by Chilton Office Supplies.

CONTENTS

LIST OF ILLUSTRATIONS

Editor's Note:

In the Introduction all Tulip quotes are either indented or in quotation marks. In chapters 2-7 all italic script indicates editorial input. Where possible the original format has been retained. Square brackets are used to replace missing words, reconstruct difficult sentences or make editorial comment where it is considered a footnote would be intrusive, e.g. personal and place names, dates and selected words or phrases. Persons mentioned in the text are not always readily identified. Often no name occurs or when it does just a surname is mentioned, thus making indexing difficult and identification tenuous - the editor accepts responsibility for any inaccuracies. The following abbreviations appear after footnotes to indicate their source, AC, Ashley Cooper; EED, English Dialect Dictionary (Ed., J. Wright, 1900); JD, John Dixey; PR, Peter Rowe; TR, Tom Rowe. Notes are provided on pages 20 and 53 for readers not familiar with pre-metric weights, measures and currency.

Map 1   BULMER IN TULIP'S TIME
Settlements, roadways and tracks

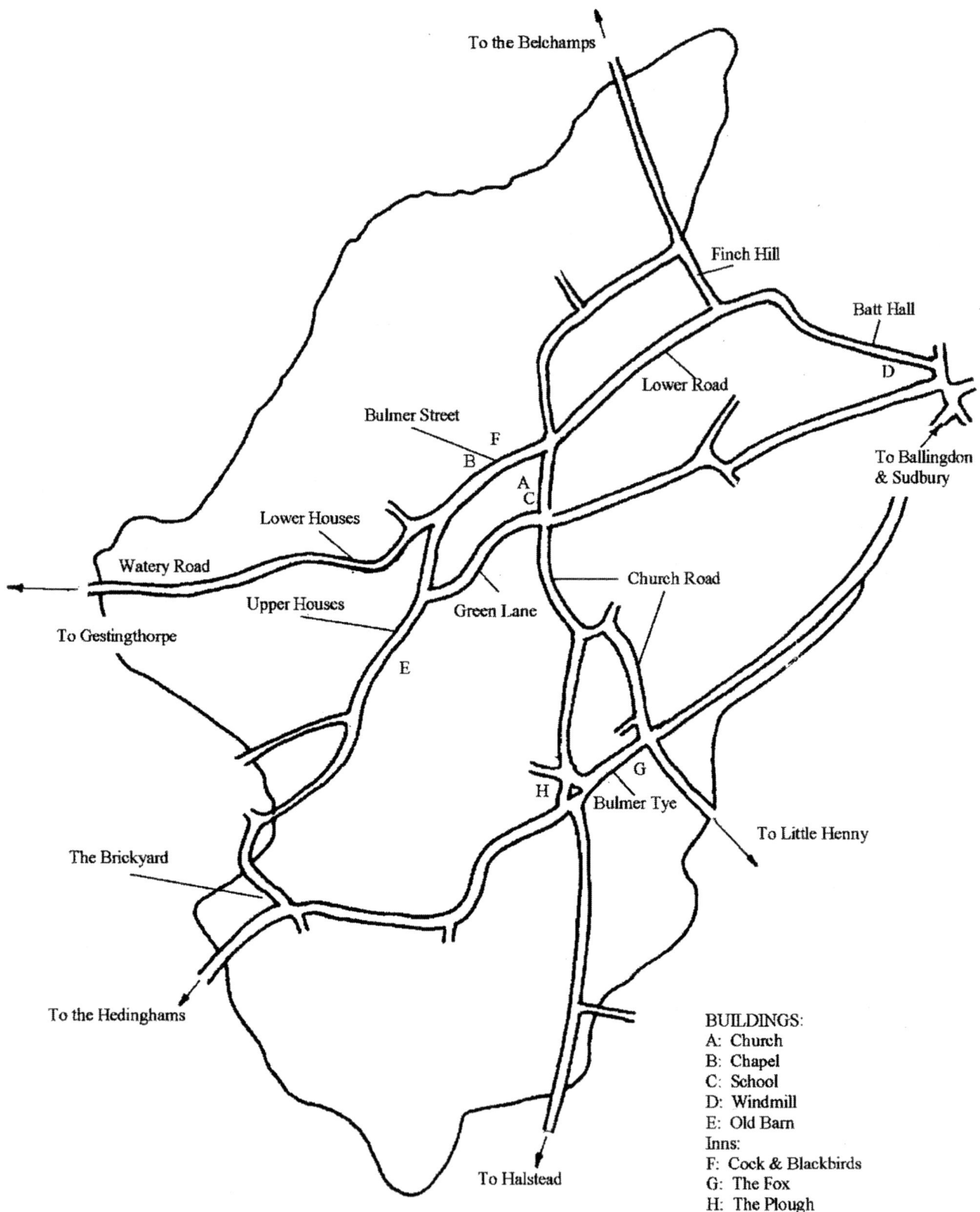

To the Belchamps

Finch Hill

Batt Hall

Lower Road

D

To Ballingdon & Sudbury

Bulmer Street

F

B

A

C

Lower Houses

Watery Road

Church Road

To Gestingthorpe

Upper Houses

Green Lane

E

G

H   Bulmer Tye

To Little Henny

The Brickyard

To the Hedinghams

To Halstead

BUILDINGS:
A: Church
B: Chapel
C: School
D: Windmill
E: Old Barn
Inns:
F: Cock & Blackbirds
G: The Fox
H: The Plough

IN TULIP'S TIME

A BULMER CRAFTSMAN'S MEMORIES

From the writings of

Philip 'Tulip' Rowe
(1871 – 1955)

Vol. I

Edited by Robin Rowe

Philip Rowe Archive – Bulmer, Essex

1. INTRODUCTION

The writings of Philip Rowe, or 'Tulip' as he was nicknamed early in his life, have been 'worked upon' for many years. It is therefore high time they were made available to the general public. A problem from the outset has been one of format and editorial license. The difficulty with the former is one of continuation and arrangement. The originals – written between 1927–28 and 1936-38 – are a mishmash of partly related topics ranging from country lore and agricultural practice to domestic procedures and severe weather narratives. All this, together with biographical comment and anecdote, is loosely connected by perambulations around Tulip's beloved parish of Bulmer in Essex. There is little evidence of formal planning:

> I do not know, or hardly, what I have [to write about] till I sit down to it, as
> at present . . . for, Reader, I do not prepare what I say to any person [even]
> if I know I have to go to see whoever it may be, neither do I prepare what I
> write – only if a subject comes into my mind when I am away from pen or
> pencil.

Written in the vernacular they display a dialectal grammar, contain errors of syntax and require, every now and again, careful sentence reconstruction to make the meaning clear. Topics are repeated from time to time, so consequently a choice has to be made between retention of the best or a splicing together of two accounts. Thus the editorial input has become a major part of the work, deciding whether to retain the original exactly as it stands, or change as little as is thought necessary to make the text flow as easily as possible. Bearing in mind that Tulip will have left the village school sometime just after his twelfth birthday to begin a life working on the land, the grammar is passable, the spelling excellent and the handwriting enviable. From time to time sentence construction has been changed and topics 'grouped' into related passages, the latter being reflected in the intention to publish the major topics, the perambulations and the natural history writings in separate volumes. The decision to make such changes has been eased by Tulip's own words:

> I hope Readers I have not repeated that I have written too much. Also I
> hope this will be worth reading [by] whosoever do. I hope that I have not
> made many misspelled words – I know there are some. Also I hope that
> any Readers who do [see] if I have missed a word or a letter, so that the
> wrong meaning is taken of that I have written will not criticise. For I have
> not read over but very little that is wrote in the books. So if wrong
> Readers, rectify if you wish or please.

The term 'writings' is used to describe the mixture of plain narrative, memoirs, anecdotes and tales; the whole being a mix of local and social history.

Tulip was born at Upper Houses, Bulmer, Essex, on 19th January 1871 and died there on 3rd of February 1955. He was an agricultural labourer and country craftsman. Sometimes working for an employer direct, sometimes for himself, but never living in a 'tied' cottage and definitely not afraid to terminate employment and seek work elsewhere. It has to be born in mind that he suffered periodically from what today would be termed nervous breakdowns. It was during the spells he spent detained under the strict internment laws of the time that the writings were produced. It has been suggested that he was encouraged

1

along these lines as part of his treatment.[i] Whether this is the case or not, it must have helped by providing an opportunity not readily available after a long day labouring in the fields. His own comments on the matter state as reasons, 'first because I like to do a something' and 'second, because I have found out that to do a something is better for me than to sit or stand or lie about idle.' Another passage endorses this; 'what I am really writing for is to while away time as it seems long to me doing nothing. I do not care [for] a lot of reading now, although I am fond of reading generally.'

It is interesting to note that whilst Tulip was engaged on his writings, other more well-known persons were diligently recording the changing countryside; H.J. Massingham (1888-1952), author of some fifty-plus related books and Thomas Hennell (1903-1945) author (*Change in the Farm* and others), artist and illustrator spring to mind. However it is doubtful whether Tulip was acquainted with their work.

It is hoped that an autobiographical essay, compiled from the writings, will be produced at a later date but a few notes here must suffice for the present. Despite his small stature, Tulip declares that he had 'always heard of the Rowes as being Big men,' and family tradition has it that they hailed originally from nearby Gestingthorpe. His love and loyalty to family was strong and his faith in the prowess of its members a matter of immense pride. He boasts, 'I do not believe that if Essex, well if England, was searched there could be found a family with [the] six brothers I have, myself and my four sons who are all men with a wife and issue.'[ii] He continues by listing their combined skills:

> [there are] those . . . [who] can draw a furrow, plough a stetch of land, mow with scythe, use axe, spade, fork . . . some do shear sheep, thatch, tie straw, cut hay, tie withy[iii] bands or use a hay press. Drive motors, traction engines, drive a binder [and] use a motor plough [and] portable saw bench; [in fact use] every kind of machine or tool on a farm – whether to cut chaff, saw, thresh wheat, barley and oats and all small seeds . . . Build a house, dig a well – not too deep, say twenty feet. Make the upper part of wagons [and] build a house on wheels to live in when away from home with a traction engine. Weave [plait] wheat[-straw], [make] ornamental rustic work with round wood from trees and underwood. Make beehives – either wood or straw. – [and] make bulrush frail baskets. [They can] keep bees, poultry, pigs, goats, dogs and cats. [Do] blacksmith's work [from] shoeing a horse to the mending of agricultural implements.

The list ends with mention of his son, Philip's attempt at brickmaking literally from scratch – i.e. digging the clay and building the necessary kilns.

Essentially Tulip was a countryman who felt his beloved Bulmer was not only there to be productive, but to be shared, protected and enjoyed by all:

> Surely it would be better if old lanes, footpaths etc were made so folk could take walks with their wives and families across fields, meadows, rivulets and woods that [are] away from roads. So they can let their children run and play about how they like if they do no damage to the crops. If those who

---

[i] On the flyleaf of book 11c (February 18th 1937) is written 'from Tulip Rowe to Dr. Turnbull.' Did this medic encourage Tulip's literary efforts?

[ii] A slight exaggeration as his brother George had no children.

[iii] Withy bands, withes or bands are twists of straw or bark used in the tying of sheaves and faggots. They are frequently mentioned in the text.

keep a dog, put a lead on the dog [when] near sheep, cows or poultry, the dog can take an airing as it should. Also mind [inform] the Master of it if spoken to. Let persons who have children amuse themselves by all means, but do not let them break hedges, dig up wild flowers, run in the corn or run over hay or clover cock[i] so to let them [the parents] down. For I do not believe there are many farmers around my part who would mind if they saw a man with his wife and his children, yes, [and] with a dog, go across a field or a meadow if they did no harm, [even] if it were not on a footpath. For there are times in a year when one can go across a field and do no harm at all to the crop if it be wheat, barley or oats - also meadows. That is to say if hedges are not broken or gates where cattle are grazing [left open] . . . with all the motor cars on the roads of today it is not a safe place on the roads, for boys and girls like a romp and should have it. I know also there are no such good walks on a road as there are in old lanes and footpaths that go over a few fields and meadows; those were the walks I used to like with my wife and four boys . . . certainly no farmer or landowner ought to begrudge poor folk of the privilege of going across their land if there is no damage done. For they can get in their cars and go miles and miles in an hour or two, to see nice things.

Books V, VI and VII detail the many wild plants known to him; the descriptions mainly practical with only a touch of the sentimental:

Ground ivy or alehoof or turnhoof is to be seen in the wood and this is a plant that likes shady places. This plant runs a long way, rooting as it goes. It is a purplish flower and looks nice when bloomed thick. This is used by some folk to clarify thick beer, for it is said to be good for that purpose . . . Hemlock will also come up in such hedges where the soil suits it. It is gathered when in bloom for some kind of drug. I gathered, with my sons, a lot two seasons for a factory. I had so much per hundredweight. It is heavy to carry to where the cart is, for one cannot get to where it grows if the fields are of corn. But it does not plant so thickly after the hedge grows up - as it is with nearly all the other kind of flowers or plants I have mentioned. Hemlock also grows in disused chalk pits and where earth has been dug for bricks etc. Hemlock grows very tall. It is poisonous, [and] not unlike a kind of parsley that tame rabbits are fond of and it has been picked for the same to the disappointment of the boys who had the rabbits for pets.

Geographically speaking Tulip's world was small, but his knowledge of that world correspondingly large. Probably the furthest he ever travelled was to London, where he stayed with friends and visited his brother Charles, a Coldstream guardsman. These visits are described in detail as are his wanderings from Severall's Hospital - desperate attempts to prove his sanity which make compulsive reading as we hear of his long treks on foot, carrying his 'coat, mac, umbrella [and] a few tools which I brought with me to earn a little money,' and covering the ground from the hospital as quickly as possible without being detected. One has to remember that Tulip was in his late fifties and sixties at these times:

. . . I eventually reached the village called Norton about 9.30 at night . . . I chanced to drop in [at The Plumber's Arms] in this time of need [of the rest] I so sorely wanted on that night of 12th October 1926. A night, in fact a day

---

[i] Small heap of hay, corn or clover in a field - EDD.

and night, for never was I so tired in my life before. How stiff and tired I was for two of three days after - God knows.

However the hardships were far outweighed by Tulip's elation at the end of the fourteen days,[i] when 'my friend drove me by <u>car</u> to my dear old native place <u>Bulmer</u>. Yes <u>My Home</u>.' *(sic)*

His descriptive passages are certainly the most lucid, but he is on shakier ground when offering personal opinions concerning his abstract thoughts and feelings. However the occasional passage borders on the poetic. From the hospital ward at Severall's:

> . . . I got up and looked at the sun as it was rising three mornings running. It was lovely, the window a little way open, the birds all round singing and two mornings out of three a lovely scent came through like sweet briar and another scent I knew well but could not recognise it. I drew a deep breath both times and it seemed to me to thrill me right through and that it was nice to be alive as it is at that time of the year [about Easter time] above all times to me.

or,

> The chestnut trees were in full leaf and blossom, looking lovely in their new green with the white pyramid of flowers. How they appealed to me.

When Tulip writes of his hospital experience, ever the practical man, he expresses amazement at the Severall's logistical operation and yet with compassion for his fellow sufferers; words of criticism are rare:

> The patients are quiet for poor chaps [and] I find more of them that I see and notice are more of a religious turn of mind than any ward I have been in yet. Not that I am in any way thinking that religion is going to get me out of here or the reverse, but I know these are the [ones who] are more comfortable [here] to my idea. I think for my own part that to do to others as you like others to do to you is the best religion and will carry us through life.

Bulmer has changed a great deal since Tulip's birth, not beyond recognition, but the many small fields, some sizable woods and a goodly number of cottages have disappeared to make room for large post-war 'prairies' and a smattering of housing estates. In 1871 the population was just beginning to decline after its maximum figure of 807 in 1851, to 733 and by the time of Tulip's death to around 500. However more significant to these Bulmer memories are the changes in agricultural topography and practices. The amenities have dwindled to one public house and one small postal outlet, but no chapel, blacksmith, wheelwright, baker or shoemaker. Tulip's recipes for brewing, baking and curing are little more than a curiosity. The Sunday lunch is no longer poached, gleaned wheat no longer flailed, sheaves have disappeared and whatever happened to the weather?

---

[i] After fourteen days away from an institution, patients regained their freedom.

2. THE DOMESTIC SCENE

The main passages in this chapter outline the importance in Tulip's mind of what George Ewart Evans has termed the three Bs – bread making, brewing and bacon curing. Incidental insights into the domestic scene are scattered amongst the writings.

Meal times and parental care

[The evening meal was called] . . . supper, for we never said tea, only on a Sunday when we had had a good cooked dinner with a bit of meat. Got a good fill – the only time perhaps we all had our dinner together and a good dinner at that. A good day to know, a Sunday. Then we called tea, 'tea' for we wanted little else unless celery or watercress or other salad. We [also] liked to push a bit of bread and butter down. Not so when I had been using a scythe all day, then walked two or three miles to get home. We wanted a supper, not tea. My father never minded talking about things before us children about house affairs or anything else that did not matter before children. But we were told not to talk of home affairs or that was said of anyone at home. Neither did we I will warrant. For if I had [talked] of other folks business and any trouble was caused by so doing [either parent] would have punished us. My father [and mother] were always doing something for the home. Neither one sat looking about them or sleeping, but in bed – not up. My mother used to make all our clothes. For father she made corduroy trousers; also jacket sleeve waistcoats. Also she made for us boys their knickers etc out of old clothes, which my two cousins would give or send to our house knowing their aunt would make the best of them. I know mother always gave a good price for corduroy.

Meal times and terms

Home-baked bread

My mother would never have a dutch-oven. She said she made out with all her family without one. [She] had to do most of her cooking by boiling, unless when she baked bread. Perhaps then if we had a piece of meat, that would be good baked. She would put it in the oven some time before the bread had to be taken out. And that she did not like to do for one should not let the steam out of the oven when baking bread or the bread might become heavy.

My mother always baked her own bread in an oven in a bake-room belonging to the owner of the cottages [at Upper Houses] – five in all. There were few labourers wives in Bulmer that did not bake bread at that time and for many years after. Formerly there was a bread oven in all five cottages. All needed repairing so a bake-house was builded instead. In the cottage now my home my wife did bake a few times. I had one built and we annealed it – having to keep a fire in for twenty-four hours. A slow fire at first to dry the bricks and floor of the oven, then a good fire to be kept burning using large logs etc. It did not matter how big and laying along the full length of the oven.

Making a bread oven

My father always did a hedge[i] if he could to get bush faggots for my mother to bake bread with. So plenty of faggots were needed for that purpose. Two a week were a good average, but sometimes three had to be used. If a few large pieces are

Faggots for the oven

---

[i] 'Taking a hedge' was a farm worker's perquisite i.e. the master's hedge was cut in return for the wood.

in a faggot [all] the better, for large wood is best if it can be burnt out for the baking of bread, as the oven does not need so much attention as [when using] small brushwood – then the oven may not be left long if the fire is very low.

The bread is much better than baker's bread – or so I think. When my mother's family was large she used to bake one week under the other. We ate very little new bread for we would soon eat up a batch. Bread is also much better [now] than in the times I went to school, especially if it were such a wet harvest as it were in 1879. I of course did not know quite as much as perhaps I do now, but I know about that time [as] we had to eat very funny bread.

Flour

The grist,[i] or gleaning and allotment wheat were sent to the grist-mill or whatever the mill was called. My uncle had the flour he baked with from there, but my father had his flour from his brother-in-law[ii] as they were relatives.[iii] One day whilst eating a meal with his mates in the collar hole[iv] father was eating his dark sodden bread that did not go down although he was hungry. He saw his mate's bread looked very white. So he said to him, "Let me taste it. That look nice to this," showing him his own. "Well," he said, "it is better than mine, not so heavy. Where do you get your flour from?" Father said, "I will try that. Then I shall have to change dealing with my sister. But I cannot help that unless they change their flour. Where do you reckon Deal's comes from?" He was told, "the Sudbury Water-mill." When the next half sack was needed for baking etc., he ordered one from Mr. Deal of Bulmer Street. What a difference! I well know I can tell you Readers. For at that time we had not too much butter put on our bread I can assure you. Also I know I did not live so hard as many more of my schoolmates did – for some of them had not enough to eat.[v] Father saw his sister and told her that he had flour off Mr. Deal and should continue to do so even if they did not. Of course they had fault found of their bread but did not like changing after so many years of dealing from the same millers. Anyhow they did change and were pleased they did so.

It was a business, [the] making of home-baked bread then. The flour was at home, but yeast had to be got and that from where it was best. For although it could be got from all brewers it could not every week, for some brewed once a fortnight. Then perhaps from some places it made the bread bitter, or it did not rise properly before being kneaded. I know of one brewery where the yeast was good for a long time, perhaps a year or two. We, either me or my sister, but not often her, had to go to Ballingdon Brewery - some two miles to take our yeast-can with our names on it plainly, on a Thursday. All ready to be collected on Friday morning with money left in the can. The cans left so were filled first and set to one side. All were filled so before the others [i.e. late comers] could start to get yeast. This was done because there were such crowds came to that brewery to get yeast because it was the best around that district. Then to keep folks out of where it was served a chain was in the door so that the cans could only be pushed in, with the money for the amount of yeast wanted. They had to be careful if all were to be served. I have

Getting yeast from Ballingdon Brewery

---

[i] Grain to be ground not milled.

[ii] James Patrick, married to David Rowe's sister Henrietta (Retty). The business is listed in Kelly's Directory 1874 & 1899. PR. Also known as Jim Theobald – see page 16-17.

[iii] The baking business was at Rose Cottage, Blacksmith's Lane, Bulmer Tye.

[iv] See page 51.

[v] Elsewhere Tulip says, 'several of my school pals who, when they went to work, had for a drink burnt bread with water poured on to give a colour that it should look like tea. It was but burnt bread tea.'

seen over forty – maybe a lot more. I know I did that until I left school, then my sister had to do it if no one else could.

I have heard sometime afterwards by the same brewers how well they did from yeast sales. Perhaps Readers it may interest you to know that brewers have at times to get a fresh stack of yeast, for beer yeast must be changed from time to time. The whys and wherefores I do not know. But yeast in liquid form is bad stuff for travelling far in bulk. It must not be in an airtight container or so [I was told by] someone who knew, or ought to, for he was in the trade. He told me that if yeast was put in a cask, which was headed up and had far to travel, and then shaken up too much, then nothing could hold it. Yeast is very messy if spilled on anything. It also smells very bad when gone off. It often surprises me how a little yeast will leaven a lot. I know it will if put in tubs of new beer.

Yeast

A yeast was used first by one and then another till it was tried … [all around] the parish. Of course all those who baked were interested, knowing what a business it was to get, for no one was sure of brewer's yeast. Of course it would leaven, but it might not rise in the trough – a wooden one four or five foot long on legs and usually made of elm. I had a new one. That has been in use for more than forty years now. It was made by J. Amos of Little Henny. It was bad for the family if the mother had the misfortune to have a bad batch of bread. Yes I have known bread to go what is called ropey. That is, if one breaks the crumb one could see little strings like a spider's web, say, inches from one crumb to another. That bread wanted some getting down unless it was put in broth – even then it would not soak. Some men when the sun shone would lay it in the sun to dry it, or toast it by the fire if at home. It would go down better then.

Importance of good yeast

Home-Brewed Beer

Readers, having mentioned yeast and beer I will now write of the making of home-brewed beer. Teetotallers crack up tea, coffee, cocoa or say minerals – I say let them drink them by all means, but why find so much fault with beer, when many say they have never tasted it. I do not believe they would have complained had they had some of it in their mother's milk, if their mother's had suckled them. If it were good homemade beer made from good hops and malt, with not too much water with it in the making, neither begrudging it wasting when boiling if they had the average amount to fill up. This was two half-hogshead[i] casks with a few gallons over to put in bottles of one to two gallons to drink before the casks were ready to broach. Which would be after it had done working, say eight or nine days. Then the bung would be put in the casks ready to put the tap in when the bottles were empty.

Of teetotallers

Well to brew a sack of malt and 5lbs of hops need a bit of doing, for it cannot be well done in a day … [father] used to get up early and boil the copper of water so he could mash up about five o'clock. For one has to get water, yes, from a long way sometimes. Around our district the majority of men that worked on farms brewed just before harvest. Farmers would lend a man a horse and water cart to get water from a good pond or spring for the occasion, although very few times did we need that. Then there was the wood to cut. Large round wood generally with a little coal is best. For with coal and wood together the water, or beer, in the copper can soon be got to boil. Then a slow fire after.

Home brewing

---

i A whole hogshead cask held over 50 gallons or 227.30 litres.

The copper is first filled with water, providing all the tubs and the mash tun is ready for use. For I know after a spell of hot and dry weather everything leaks that is of wood. So these have to be stenched-wetted from time to time to get the staves of the tubs to swell close so they will hold liquid. It takes quite a time for them to do so at times unless they can be put into a pond etc. First the water is boiled, then put in the mash tun with cold water added, for if malt is scalded it will turn like a batter and it will not run off. The fine malt must not dumple[i] up or it cannot be wetted, so the malt is let slowly into the tun, one stirring all the time. If there is not quite enough water more boiling water is added from the copper. This is the first 'wort'.[ii] It is stirred well and then covered up for four hours or a little less to get it ready for the 'second wort'. The first is drawn out to a low tub generally called an 'under bank'. That will not hold all, so a wort tub[iii] is brought out to hold the surplus. Enough water is then taken out of the copper for the second wort.

Problems with leaky tubs

The first wort is then put into the copper quickly so that the copper does not burn. The second wort is stirred well and then covered up for the four hours whilst the first wort is being boiled. Hops were put into the copper as soon as there was enough wort in the copper to wet them. The hop grows wild in several places in the parish, in hedges near springs or wet ditches. These trail a long way about the hedges and have some lovely hops on in some seasons. I have picked them to make home-brewed beer. All the first wort was put into the copper to boil till the four hours were up and when the second wort was ready to come off.

Local hops

The first wort is called Sweet Wort, nice to drink a little of, being very sweet. It is also good to make vinegar – the very best, although we never made it. When the first wort is taken out, it is put through a wicker basket called a strainer. Yes beer will not go through this after it has been used for some years – it then has to be knocked for the beer to go through. It makes me think of a man who once brewed at some neighbour of his. He found that everything in the way of tubs and mash tun leaked. He told someone that "everything runned except the strainer". And I know that is a job to get beer through after being used a number of times.

Sweet wort

After two worts are made into beer this is put into two tubs for working. When it is cool enough, for it will not work if too hot or cold – luke-warm is best – yeast is added and stirred well in. Soon if it is working there is a good crop of yeast on the two tubs. Then after a day this new yeast is taken off and the beer put into casks to be used when needed. It is not long before the taps can be put in. If the malt and hops are good, then this is good to drink as soon as it has settled down again.

It is quite fit to drink. Yes, good to take into the fields where one cannot get home to dinner. Nothing better, and I know if one has hard work to do if he drinks a pint of that it is better than tea, coffee or cocoa to work with. And one could drink a good lot before it would muddle any man at any kind of work, if used, as beer should be, not for the sake of drinking.

The following extract by Tulip gives another glimpse into the use of wooden

---

[i]   Get lumpy – EDD.
[ii]   The first wort gave strong beer, whilst the second wort produced mild or small beer.
[iii]   See Fig 5 page 43.

containers. Kelier appears to be the Essex dialect word for Keeler.

If the weather was fine, that was when the boys[i] had to go in the hoops as we called it. This was a large bath we had. If not the wash-kelier was used. A kelier was a low tub with a wide ashen loop made for the top to lift it about by and good things too to wash their clothes in. [There were] very few iron or tinned things[ii] in the early days. Many wooden pails were used for drinking water to be fetched and stand in. Galvanised pails were not good for water to stand in. Beer that had aged was even worse. Folks were ill if they drank old ale out of these pails.

Of wooden tubs

Of Meat and the curing of Ham

Only on a Sunday did many a family get a piece of meat. I know I have been glad to get a taste of rabbit on a Sunday. And that was a tame rabbit that perhaps my father bought – or a pair of them – to get big and fat so it could be killed to spare going to the town to get a piece of meat. [Often] it was too rough for my father to go. For my mother could not and the shop things we needed were fetched by neighbours with theirs. So father would not trouble them to bring a piece of meat from the butchers. Also my father managed to kill two pigs twice each year. He was a thrifty man as also was my mother and we children always had to do something for the house and home. Also for ourselves if we were to have luxuries, I can tell you. For we went to gleaning, picking up acorns and running errands for our neighbours if they wanted us. Of course they always gave us something for so doing – a penny or two or a bit of cake. Also my sister and me did pick up stones on the farm my father worked a year or two before I left school. This would be after we got home from school, say from the middle of March into April, or before the corn was up. I know one Saturday my sister and me picked up twenty bushels of stones in a field near our house. We never picked up so many more in one day. I know we both had a new pair of shoes from stone picking. Father told us that he was as pleased as we were of it. I have known acorns to sell for 1/6 per bushel and for them to take twenty bushels from our house at a time. Also I have seen them go for 1/- per bushel - and folk were pleased to get 1/- for them. I knew a man with a young family and they picked up enough acorns one season to pay for shoes all round for them.

Stone picking

New shoes

Acorning

I mentioned pigs. My father's pig court had bricks on the bottom, for he cleaned it out as it was too near the house by law. But the inspector who had to do with nuisances said, "Rowe, as I always find your pigs clean I shall not give an order to remove them, for it is a good pigsty and you keep it clean." So it was always kept. He used to have them killed by my uncle. We liked that time too for we had plenty of meat. Perhaps a fortnight or more of fresh pork. The pigs pluck was cut up so all the neighbours had a taste of it or some other little bit they liked, as was the custom. Four or five out of our ten [dwellings] [at Upper Houses] kept a pig or two. These were killed to pay the rent by some. I know a man was looking at one of our neighbour's pigs once when G. H. [?] said to him, "Here's my rent," pointing to the pig. "How mate would it be if he died?" Came the reply. "I had not thought of that," he said.

Keeping pigs at home

If my father kept two pigs he always sold one, keeping the other for himself or not selling more than a quarter out of it – whether it was a fore or hind quarter. This

---

[i] *Tulip and his brothers.*
[ii] Utensils and implements.

9

three-quarters was cut so the bones were cut out thus: the two spare ribs from neck to loin and from the loin bones to the tail. These were cut with not too much fat on them. The back fat was put in a tub of wood called a pork tub. This was much bigger below than at the top. Good for putting down pork to be salted, for the pork should, or must be, covered with liquid brine. Loin bones and spare ribs nowadays are usually cut out with thick fat over them. The rule when salted pork was needed was just to take the bones out of the fat. There is then plenty of fat on the spare rib as well as the loin so it can be cooked well. We also used to salt the two breasts, one from each side and also part of the flank from the hindquarters.

Salted pork

Of the two hands one can cut off the pieces to fry for a time or boil or pickle with sweet brine as we always did, my father and mother for their family, me and my wife for us. Both of our two families had pigs done in this way. I used to put more down to sweet pickle, as my sons did not care so much for salted pork as my brothers and sisters. So I put down the two faces or chaps of the pig, the two hands that are the shoulder part of the foreleg, the two breasts and the two legs behind. We made the sweet pickle as follows. If say a leg weighs sixteen pounds, then we used one pound of salt and one pound of Barbados or black sugar. These two pounds could be mixed together and put in an earthen pot or pan. A pint of stout or beer is added. The pieces were rubbed or floated in such brine – turning the thin pieces from time to time – for a month or so. Afterwards they were taken out and dried. We put them up a chimney, a large one, in paper bags to protect from the soot. The legs were kept in the pickle for six weeks.

Sweet pickle

Self-sufficiency!

Yes Readers I can say for myself [that] from the time I got married [in December 1896] till The Great War was on, we both had home-brewed beer, salt pork, hams and bacon. Soon after, one could not kill a pig or brew without a permit.

The Jennens estate

There were numbers of farms in many parts around Long Melford that belonged to the Jennens Estate, afterwards Earl Howe's.[i] This gentleman had a lot of cottages besides [as well as] the farms. Some of the farms had a cottage or two that went with them, all paying rent to the agent of Earl Howe. All these were let at 1/- per week with a pigsty built for the pig to sleep and sty. There are I know, three such in Bulmer.[ii]

Gleaning

Gleaning bell

Pigs were sent into the fields to 'shack' as it was called. That is to pick up the corn – short ears of barley, for wheat was gleaned in those days. The church bell used to be tolled every morning at eight o'clock and again at six o'clock in the evening and no one was allowed to go gleaning either before or after the bell went.

Of gleaning, yes I have seen forty or more women and children waiting outside in the road when the rakings were being carted away. I know one day I went with my mother to a field called Tollgate Field. An old Italian [appeared] who carried an organ on his back. One of the gleaners, an old lady, asked him to play a tune. He stopped and looked around to see if others were going to agree that he should.

---

[i] The Bulmer farms were, Griggs or Swains, Butlers Hall, Black House, Jenkins, Kitchen and Tye Corner.
[ii] Two cottages that had these sties were a pair of thatched cottages opposite Bulmer Chapel – 'Langley Cottage' and 'Warlin' – the last being pulled down in 1995 – PR.

Someone said, "Can we get some money for him if he do play?" Them who had a penny or two on them gave, so it made a start for something to give him. He played a few tunes, perhaps all of them the organ could play. Anyhow the last wagon was coming out of the field so all soon started to glean.

I know my mother had a nice lot to take home, but not a head bundle. That was a bag made of calico, fairly wide. When full it was tied up at the top. Then to carry this the women carried it on their heads. Yes, and heavy too if cut off short near where the handfuls were tied. But sometimes when it was hot and dry and the straw was brittle it could not be tied with straw. Some would twist long grass or anything that would tie the handful. For if kept in handfuls more could be put into the bags. One scarcely saw anything in a field but white bags. Also a smaller bag *Gleaning bags* was tied round the waist. This was to put the short ears of wheat in. This bag was called a chob bag.

In some fields then there were good gleaning. Of course I did not then know the *The young* reason. But once I heard this. The young ladies of the Auberies[i] once visited an *ladies mistake!* old lady in the parish – these ladies did I know visit many of the cottages – and this lady who these visited told them [that she and others] did like gleaning in their father's fields because there was always such good gleaning there. Good old dear! Of course the ladies liked to know their father thought so well of the poor. They told him what the old lady had told them. Of course not to blame the gentleman either. He blamed the bailiff for having so much corn lying about, what he had to pay good Money [*sic*] to have got in from the wheat fields. These he had had plowed [*sic*],[ii] harrowed, rolled perhaps first, then harrowed again before he drilled the wheat in the said ground. He then had to roll, harrow, hoe, weed etc before it was cut – to cut perhaps with a scythe or sickle and then [at a later time] no doubt a machine. It had to be tied by hand, [then] shocked, stoked or traved - as it is called in places, [but] all [meaning] the same thing. Afterwards threshed with machine, not frail - [of which] I wrote before[iii] – and then taken from the machine to the barn to be dressed.

When all the gleaning was over those who gleaned paid the old lady who tolled the church bell. Women who had families where say three or four were small, took them into the fields to glean. For mothers would take their suckling babes in the field. Thought nothing of sitting on her gleaning bag to give the little dear her tit, which would often be seen. I know my brothers did for they would soon make Mother hear if they did want it.

I know in the year 1879 it was a very late harvest. On the farm Jenkins they did *Very late* not begin until 1st September. I know a field of seventeen acres, where the rakings *harvests* were not carted and a shock [was left standing as a sign] for gleaners not to go in till it was 5th November or after. For we went to see [this], me and my sister. I know very well. Very late and the harvest was not finished on that farm till after November 5th. I have heard both my cousins say of the same.

---

[i] Miss Rachel Edith (b1843) and Miss Alice (b1847), daughters of James Burke. Rachel was a member of Bulmer's first Parish Council – both lived at 'The Cedars' – now 'The Dower House' – JD.

[ii] There are few spelling errors in the originals, but 'plow' is Tulip's common spelling for ' plough' – this has been retained where it occurs .

[iii] See pages 47 – 48.

Storing the gleanings

The corn was taken home and put in the house. Ours was a large old house with a garret where I slept the most, up in the wind beams as we called them. The principles, builders call them. I know one could get a knock if they did not walk carefully, even if not tall. So there was plenty of room to put the corn when dry, for the wheat ears had to be thoroughly dry before it was put away.

Threshing in the home

Well of course Reader the folk who had this corn had to thresh it out. It had to be done by frail,[i] for the same to go through a threshing machine driven by steam power or [as] now by motor engine, is another matter. Plenty of threshing was done in homes. One thing was for flour, but poor folk could not buy a cloth as one can nowadays or get bags or sacks either. I know that well enough. How the men used to thresh with flail in such low rooms as some were I know, I could not make out. For I did some in an empty house adjoining ours, but that was 8ft 3ins or the height of half a rod or pole. There has been plenty threshed in that, but not in my time. I have heard my father say one of his neighbours threshed three sacks of wheat – of allotment corn and gleaned wheat - in a day and fanned it ready for the mill. The room in his cottage was cleared and the corn laid out on the flour and threshed. The room is not more than seven feet high - a lot of difference to a barn. But it was a very long day from early morning till nearly midnight - a long day for all in the house, for it was turned upside down as the saying is. For to thresh corn is a dusty job, for the rain splash the grit onto the wheat ears after it is cut and it lay on the ground. Nowadays it is taken to a threshing machine and put through – not too fast. Then if it is Rivet Wheat, the Bearded or Great Wheat, it is a hard matter to get all the corn out of the ears, for it is very tough to thresh at any time and short ears are likely to go through whole. The fan belonged to a man Deal, who was father to the church clerk. He bought it, and then something was given to him by those who used it. The chaff would be sold. Folk who kept a pony or donkey would buy it. One day a man who kept a pony found when cleaning it something in the way of the currycomb. He, feeling for the obstacle felt a needle. He got a pair of pincers and pulled it out. It was a darning needle. He supposed that was in the gleaning chaff.

Ballingdon Mill

Well the grist or wheat would be taken from the house to the mill – a smock or cap mill - the one that stood in Ballingdon – the house in Bulmer. A man who drove the miller's cart, John Mears, used to come for it and bring it back for 1/- or the miller had the bran and toll.[ii] I think it was the price.

Straw Plaiting

Straw plaiting was carried out in north Essex as a cottage industry from about 1790, when it is said to have been introduced at Gosfield by the first Marquess of Buckingham. It is unlikely that this Essex industry was ever a serious rival to the east Midland trade centred in Luton and Dunstable, but it was nevertheless a thriving concern and remained so well into the C19. It is estimated that 'more than half the working females of Bulmer in 1871 did straw plaiting, one hundred and one plaiters out of one hundred and seventy at work.[iii] Bulmer also had its plaiting schools. Two are remembered, one at the Tye and the other at Dairy

---

[i]   Flail, where Tulip uses the dialect form, 'frail' this is retained. For illustration see fig 8, page 68
[ii] Toll was a measure of grain retained by the miller for the privilege of dealing with his mill – it varied from one establishment to another – a quart being retained for a bushel and a bushel for a quarter and so on. A 'handful' was also a term used, as was a 'toll-dish'. See *The Local Historian's Glossary of Words and Terms* – Bristow – 2001.
[iii] *Bulmer Then and Now*, Ed., Basil Slaughter, 2nd edition 1990.

Farm Cottages.[i] *Apart from hat making for home use – as in the case of David Rowe's wife Eliza, cited below – virtually all plait found its way to the east midland centres for making up.*

At the time I am writing of folk grew wheat on their allotments not only for corn, but [also] for the straw they needed for plaiting or braiding.[ii] I will only tell of father's allotment. He used to grow one third of that wheat. This he cut with a scythe and tied up into sheaves. The straw was cut to leave a fare high stubble, for the top part of the straw is best for plait - also the joints are further apart than near the ground where the stem is hard and not fit for the work. In this way it is also kept straight for it is not good if it were bent.

Allotment wheat for plaiting

The sheaves were put into one or two shocks and flags were put on to frighten the sparrows, for Mr. Jim [the sparrow] like wheat kernels. They will also go for a small piece of wheat [rather] than a large field away from the farm. As soon as dry enough these sheaves were taken home and prepared. Mother if she could, would do some or help. A sheaf was untied, laid down and a handful taken out. This was combed out with a short piece of rake to remove the flag and bindweed. The ears were pulled down all level and tied with a few straws that had been damaged - as such straw is tough and does not break on tying. After a lot of handfuls were ready father had a scythe off the handle. The point of the blade was pressed into some wood or a door and with the cray-end [or handle-end] pressed against his body he cut these handfuls off close to the ears or an inch or two away. The ears were collected for threshing later. The straw was then put into handfuls of ten or more straws and tied ready to be used or sold. Father would tie up eight or nine handfuls in one tight bundle and store out of the way in a dry place. We used a garret for this purpose but many cottagers had to keep it in a bedroom. A bundle of straw would fetch a shilling. Some years it was no trouble to get rid of. I have known a man come from Gestingthorpe, three miles or so away, and take three or four bundles away at a time. Plaiting straw fetched about a shilling for a bundle of about a dozen handfuls.

Preparing straw for plaiting

Although my mother was not the best of straw plaiters I have known her do some. There was a lot of processes to go through before it could be taken to Ballingdon to be sold. For plaiting, the bundle was untied and the straws stripped for plaiting one at a time. It was nearly cut through at a joint and with a jerk the flag would slip off. The straw under the flag being the whitest and brightest. These were laid carefully in a heap until enough was ready to be stoved or bleached. The straws were placed in a box into which was placed a tin or jar containing lumps of brimstone or sulphur. This was set alight and the lid was let down. The sulphur fumes bleached the straw.

Plaiting

Then a small bone instrument was used called an engine. This had a sharp point and a lot of clogs, teeth or sharp notches, six, seven or eight. The point was thrust into the hollow of the stem to split it. These engines were made out of a good solid bit of bone cut with a file - the wings according to order. Some were made with a small hole through to put a small haft into; others had a sharp piece of bone on the top to put into the haft. I had several at one time, which I found in a box

Plaiting 'engines'

---

[i] Now demolished.

[ii] Tulip uses both 'plaiting' and 'braiding', although the most usual form is 'plaiting'.

that I bought at an auction sale. I know I gave a few away to show or as mementos.[i]

The splits were rolled to soften and make them pliable for use. The plait being made only with the best and brightest straws. When plaiting they stopped using the fine straw as soon as the straw was not of the right colour. After the plaiting was made it had to be clipped where the straws were used up and another set in, these were about an inch long. After being clipped the braid was rolled and measured on a half-yard board. A complete turn round being one yard.

Selling plait

The plait or braid was sold in scores of yards - how many for a full length I do not know, but I have several times taken it to a house in Ballingdon Street, the Essex side of Sudbury. Plenty was sold at 6d per score yards,[ii] some upwards to a shilling. There were at least four or five kinds of braids, some very intricate. Not many could do these ones. Each had a name. There was one kind called 'herring bone'. A lot of work there is to do to make very good plait, but people were glad to get a little in that way in those days.

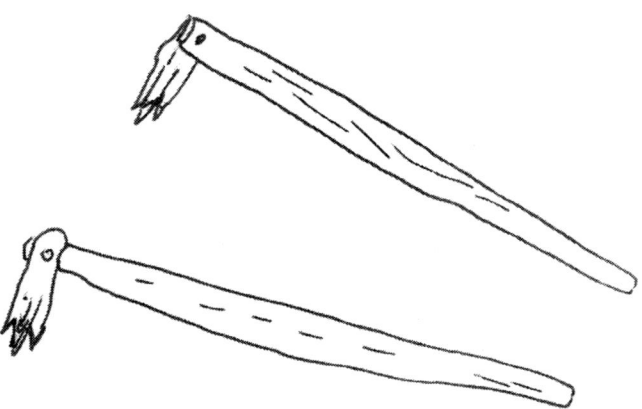

Fig 1: Plaiting Engines or Straw Splitters - approx 8–12 cm in length.

Social implications of plaiting

If a young woman was out of service she could earn a little money by straw plaiting. People that had time to braid and those that had small families and could sit down to it earned several shillings per week that way. In the next parish to Bulmer there were young men that stayed at home and earned more money in a week than if they worked for a farmer. But that was a little time before I knew of, for the plaiting was going out of date from the time I am writing about. Now there is not any done.

Straw hats

My mother used to make straw hats for father and good ones too, to wear in the summer. My father has often told me that it was handy where the wives did braiding. But it was the farmers that reaped the benefit in the long run. For had there not been plaiting, folk could not have lived at all, so folk that had the land and property would have had to give more money in wages.[iii]

---

[i] Those illustrated in Fig 1, page 14 are believed to have come from the box mentioned here.

[ii] Bundles of 40 or 50 score were the normal size sold to the plait dealer or in the markets.

[iii] For a full account of the social implications of the industry see *A History of the Straw Hat Industry*, J.C. Dony, 1942.

3. POACHERS AND KEEPERS

Judging by the proliferation of writing about poaching and keeping in countryside literature it is no surprise to find a number of references to these 'crafts' in Tulip's work. These not unbiased accounts leave us in no doubt about his personal view of the poacher-keeper scenario. Tulip's personal awe of the poacher is summed up in his comment about his great grandfather, Tom Bocking, "a poacher of the highest class."

The farmers who farmed the land over which Col. Meyrick[i] had the shooting rights did not mind if their men got the game if they did not bring their master into trouble. My Uncle [Charles] said that at that time no licence was required for a gun. Then anyone could carry one, but not for game of course. The landlord of The Plough [Mr. Parsons] had land of his own right - four acres of wood and some little fields here and there. He would not let Col. Meyrick have his shoot, he wanted that himself. So with all the keepers there were about this caused a lot of squabble. In the wood belonging to Mr Parsons[ii] a man saw a hare in a snare or the hare on a form. He did not shoot it or take it from the snare for hares were game. So the man told Mr Parsons as he knew the keepers were watching the hare. Mr Parsons said, "Well they will not hurt me as it is my land." He went on and got the hare, but had to pay a fine. They were nearly sure he did not renew his licence the first day. They were Cleaver [*sic*]. I do not suppose he lost much money over that or rest, but the other side did not gain much money over that or game through his having to pay. I will warrant they lost a lot by the transaction.

Col. Meyrick of the Auberies

Mr. Parsonss, landlord of The Plough Inn, Bulmer Tye

In two cottages [on or near the site of Bonnets Farm] lived two men. One was a keeper, a Bulmer man, the other a farm worker named March who was good at taking a rabbit and hare etc, as of course [was] his neighbour. One day this March saw a hare make a form and sit down. Thinking the coast was clear he went home for his gun. His neighbour he saw shaving at the back window and he said to himself, "I shall be alright this time I think, he will not finish shaving before I get the hare." Of course he kept his eyes open. So had the one who was shaving - for he left his job to see what March had come home for. He felt sure for his gun, for March had leave to carry it from whom he worked. The keeper followed up without being seen as far as possible. But he was seen by the gunman who shot. The keeper ran up expecting a hare or something to do with him, [but] saw the hare running in the distance. Of course he asked March if he shot at the hare. He told him, "Not this time. It was something else I shot at. But I did not stop that." I have heard my father say that he told him it was a near put that time, but he saw the keeper in the nick of time. For that hare would have been his. But what he shot at would not have been of use to either of them. What it was I was not told. It might have been a stone or a clump of grass that looked like a rabbit till one was close enough - for the gun had been pointed at something not alive.

Bonnets Farm, [near Butlers Hall]

The hare that got away!

Of course it was keepers who made a lot of bother as they usually do where game is thought too much of. For if anything goes wrong with the young pheasants it is not much trouble to put the blame on the one who happens to let a cow or bullock go near. It would be that party to blame. Also if a man went across a field when the shooting season is in. Why? If a farm worker goes across a field and there is a

Difficult keepers

---

[i] Lived at the Auberies until 1845.
[ii] Coincidentally in Parson's wood which was most likely named after the wood allocated to the Abbess of Bruisyard, Suffolk, in 1425. See *Bulmer Then and Now*, page 32.

shoot on that day the day's shooting is spoiled. If the keeper happens to see him he would tell the man that and not be civil in the telling him of it. Then if the master were a Col. Meyrick that man would get into trouble. I have seen keepers and some of their ways. But thank God I lived in a cottage independent of an Estate where game was thought so highly of.

I know I [once] harvested [at] a little farm, Clapp's Farm, and to get to it was more than a mile the nearest [way using a] footpath. If I had to keep to road or lane this would be two, and more near three [all the way] by road. So if I were working in these fields I either cut across a field and down a hedge or down a hedge and across another. Both short cuts. So if the corn were cut it was easy going. The keeper had told me in the springtime saying, "Phillip I do not mind one crossing a field this time of year, but I do not like them to go by the hedges as the birds are laying."

"Alright I do not want any of those kind of eggs [even] if I do see them," I said.

"I know but some do." Well after helping with the corn in these fields I went that way again. He met me one night saying, "You will come this way then Phillip?"

"Yes certainly. If I am working so near my house you do not wish me to go so far round as you know the other [way] is, do you?"

"No it is not that."

"Well", I said, "Do you think that I am fool enough to interfere with any of your stuff if I am glad to make a short cut?"

"No," he said, "But if you were to see anything in a snare or trap you would take it."

"That I should if I saw no one was looking. It would hurt me to have to leave it. And so it would you too," I said.

"Well you are not far out."

So I told him I should come [that way] if working those fields. One day when I was working on another farm not far from where he was talking to me, he came and stood by me a few minutes seeing that I was doing - digging a furrow just over pipes in a ditch to let water off the land. He said, "Phillip, I often hear a gun go off your way. I do not know who it is, but so-and-so mentioned their names. I wish you would let me know if you see anything."

"Mr –" I said, "I shall not [tell] of neighbours or anyone else unless it was a Duty and I was paid for the job, although I [might] live next door. It is dark when I turn out, also when I get home. I hardly ever see [anyone] either. Do I would not tell against if I did."

"I thought so of you," he said.

Well is it wrong? I cannot see that it is. He left me then.

My Uncle James was a night Ranger - one for Col. Meyrick, who had a Head Keeper who was burnt in Effigy by Bulmer folk. Besides being out in daytime the keepers had to go round at night to see that the rangers were at their post. These rangers were paid 1/- per night. A man, a keeper of Borley, was on [duty] the same night as my Uncle Jim. He was at his post. This man, Steward, by name, either crept up to my uncle or made uncle think he were a poacher. Whatever he thought my uncle closed with him and knocked him about until he said, "Oh pray Theobald don't do that". Of course my uncle had given it to him. He was carpeted for being so rough with the man Steward. But he was let off after [it was known that] it was Steward's own fault for to do what he did to see if my uncle was

16

staunch. If he had belonged to Bulmer he would have found out if Jim Tebbald[i], as they [the Theobalds] were called for shortners, [*sic*] [was staunch or not]. That family did not flinch townsfolk when they were in the town of Sudbury, for the silk weavers of Sudbury counted themselves a lot above farm labourers. If [the labourers] went to town and were near the taproom fire, these silk weavers, who earned good money, would try to hustle the countrymen. Well, this Jim and one of his younger brothers once were in the way of a lot of silk weavers, who tried to push one [of the brothers] away from the fire so as to stand in front of the fire themselves. It did not come off with these two brothers. They soon cleared the deck and had the fire to themselves, also some beer from the landlord for the two brothers and one or two other countrymen who were sitting in the back

Tension between Sudbury weavers and country folk

The Glemsford Poachers

The Glemsford folk were a rough lot I can vouch for. The place was called little Hell and they were Dears [*sic*] those I knew. I had little to do with them, but I have worked there and have had somewhat to do with Glemsford people nearly ever since I left school. These mat weavers[ii] had little recreation between them in the large village, although a man or two there had a fair with roundabouts, swing-boats etc. These men worked early and late, earning good money according to [*sic* - as compared with] farm workers, for there were some very good land and farmers around Glemsford. Well, [as] the weavers did not work on Saturdays, they had to do something for recreation. They did, for they were poachers of the poachers. For they, in their numbers going out on Saturdays and Sundays with plenty of money in their pockets for beer, would take long walks around with a dog or two. If the dogs put up a rabbit that runned to ground one of them had a ferret in their pocket. This was put in the hole. If a small hole a line was put on the ferret. One or two of the party on scout to see if anyone was coming who knew them, to let those know who was after the rabbit. If [so] … they waited till the coast was clear, then they had the rabbit if possible.

Poaching as a recreation

It was said they had a club between them. So if they were caught and given a penalty or fine it was paid out of the funds. I am only writing of that I have been told by more than one, although I quite believe it was so. I know a gang came as far as Bulmer and walked over Smeetham Hall and Goldingham Hall, because I have seen them myself. Although I never had anything to do with the party myself or with those who I know did, I have had a drink with the Glemsford folk and those who belonged near to Bulmer or in it. I have seen them from a distance walking across a large field, just as sportsmen do for the beaters, to drive the birds over the hedge whilst the guns were at their stand, ready for the birds to come up for the guns. Also I have known the bailiff and his son who told them to clear off. The only notice they took was told both of them they would be better at their breakfast than "looking after us." The what [*sic*] surprised me the most was they did the same for several Sundays. There were two keepers on one farm belonging to the Auberies as well as a policeman in the parish. Yet these men did not get taken or it seemed as if it were not known. Anyway nothing I heard of was ever done to stop them.

The Glemsford Poachers Club!

Moonlight poaching by the Glemsford men

---

[i] See note ii page 6.
[ii] See *The Matmaker and the Magistrate*, Richard Deeks, 1980.

They also came moonlight nights when the snow was on the ground, for they were seen by the tracks, beside [people] hearing the noise of the guns they had. I know [once] I was killing or helping to kill some pigs at Gestingthorpe [and] we were talking of the episode to the shopkeeper who was having the pigs killed by my mate. This house was an Off-Licensed house where one could have beer to drink off the premises, [but] of course we could [drink at the place] with pig killing. He said a Belchamp policeman told him once, not long before, of these Glemsford sportsmen. He was on duty at Seven Forms in Walter Belchamp [where grew] a very large oak with huge limbs on it, hollow so a man can stand inside without being seen on dark nights. This road leading from Sudbury to the three Belchamps is the way to come for the three. Turning right above a steep hill to St.Pauls and Otten Belchamp and straight on or turning by another road to Belchamp Walter Church and the village of Belchamp Walter. There is not a house near the road for upwards of four miles. A great part of the way is between a high bank and a hedge. Both sides thickly [planted] with plenty of fir trees. So to travel these roads it is very dark if nearly night and the moon is not showing. At about this large oak is a culvert[i] that sometimes is flooded to a depth, hence the name Severn Forms, as there were so many planks to walk on when in flood. After the culvert was made the forms were not necessary. But there is a flood if the culvert get blocked up - for a great rush I have seen at these roads. The one to Foxearth goes by way of old lanes and this narrow road that leads directly over the culvert to Foxearth, Pentlow, Glemsford etc. This tree were a meeting place for Bulmer, Belchamp and Foxearth police. One night when three of these policemen were there - to part again soon or at a given time - three men came by in the road with dogs. These said, "Good-night mates." They turned up this road called Hoe Lane. The policeman [telling the tale] had to go that way on his beat, the other two, one back to Bulmer the other by way of Borley. This policeman said we asked each other what was best to do in the case - follow them or not. They had to be at another point at a [set] time [and] what could they do with three men who perhaps were as good men as themselves. Also the three men had long dogs with them. They said, "Let them go." The one policeman had to go up this road to another point. The Hoe Lane up where he had to go is narrow and bordered thickly with trees that grow to a great height. This policeman told that it was not a comfortable walk - not a house within a mile. The nearest but a large house, Easton Hall, with a bungalow that was near half a mile off and not many living there, [but] a man and wife. He was alone with three strong young men poaching, who he might or might not come across in a little way. Presently he heard a low whistle. A hare banged into a net with dogs behind and one man after the hare. The other two standing near - less than twenty yards away from him. Those he could not see, for if he had it was too dark to recognise them. He said, "Good-night." They, "Good-night mate." He felt much better then - he was passed them. They did not wish to harm him he knew. Neither did he tell this tale till just before he was leaving to go to another place.

These Glemsford chaps be they what they may, I knew they were poachers. Yes they did well too, not often [being] taken. But most folks know that where the shoe pinches there is pain. As with them, also with keepers and others. One incident is this of one of the folk. He was out one day somewhere in Suffolk. The place or names I do not say, although I may know both or I may not. His dog caught a hare and before he could make a start a man came to him - told him he wanted the hare. "So do I," said the man who had got the hare. The [gamekeeper]

Severn Forms,
Belchamp Walter

Police predicament

Hoe Lane,
Belchamp Walter

Easton Hall

Poacher-keeper
conflict

---

[i] see note on page 32.

18

thought he was man enough to take it away. He tried to but was not man enough. The poacher, if one like to call him one, did not let him take the hare, but he took a thrashing off him and he had a sore hide. So the man to escape the law, as the gamekeeper knew him and also where he came from, went to Canada. He did well. Also he came from there three or four times to see his old pals and relatives who has told me from time to time that he did well in Canada. Good [man] too, for he was the part I knew him. If anyone needed help he would [oblige] one way or another, whether they were relatives or not. Well enough of this, but readers do not think too bad of poachers then or now. They did it for a recreation. Nothing else good around them unless sport, for they were at their looms five day out of seven. They wanted exercise. That is how they had it.

Poacher emigrates to Canada

Justice and Country Law

[After Tulip's father lost his arm] . . . a coal merchant who had formerly lived in the parish . . . went to see our squire of the parish and told him of father. Soon after, my Dad had a job being under-keeper, or help [at the Auberies]. He did the job for about four years under two keepers. He did the best he could both to his master and to those who were after his master's game. [In order that the latter should not be prosecuted] he showed himself, so if they were after game or game eggs they knew it would be best not to let father see them. For my father was a man who was not afraid, but he did not like anything that was not right for all parties. He told me many times that he did not like the job, but must do something, for keepers are not liked by folk who get things on the cheap. If a pheasant that cost a lot of money to bring up ought to be left alone, [then] a wild rabbit ought not to be the means of getting anyone to prison if it is knocked down in a road or footpath without a gun or dog and ferrets. But I do not think it right to take game eggs or the birds, for they like their nest and it certainly seem un-sportsman-like to take birds eggs to cook. But if keepers can take them to put under hens to rear them up and will buy eggs off their neighbour's land and buy eggs other than from game farms, it certainly do not ought to be a crime say for me or anyone to take eggs and sell them where they are bought and reared. Which is the more wrong? They are both wrong. For the receiver is as bad as the thief. So are they that buy game eggs in the same way, and plenty of the like is done. In the [breeding] season my father had to sit up all night to keep the fox away from the young pheasants - they had a hut to be in. If a fox was after the birds the hen would make a noise and the dog would bark. Then they would look around to see what was the cause of the commotion. For keepers are not sure that they may have human foxes and it would be no trouble to sell the young birds to those who rear them, for they do not often have too many birds.

Tulip's father, David, as an under-keeper

Views on removing eggs and rearing birds

Gamekeepers, like policemen were not liked in those days I can assure you. I quite know the reason. Also I was old enough then to see that both police and gamekeepers were of the same stamp. For although police were paid by the County they also helped to keep the game for the squire as well as the gamekeeper. The squire paying the gamekeeper and him giving the policeman a brace of rabbits or a few pigeons. Also in a big shoot he would get a pheasant or two or a hare. What for? Because he helped the keeper all he could. Yes looking out for poachers, for they must not have too many rabbits, or the keeper would not give him a brace so often. [Once] a policeman went to live [in a new area]. He did not like the place, neither did his wife after being living in a town. The squire of the place, not Bulmer, Reader, soon after sent for the policeman for he was a magistrate. Told him he hoped he would be after the fellers about there for they

Gamekeepers and policemen are alike!

19

were very good at taking rabbits off his land. The policeman could put in a word here, "Sir," he said, "I have never had to take game keeping into my duty yet. I shall not here unless my Superior tells me. I did not know it came into County Police regulations." That policeman was away from the parish within a month.

Yes what a difference in times. Perhaps it is needed. I have known the keepers of an estate in early spring go out and look over the places, woods, plantations, anywhere to see if a place was drawn by a rabbit to have her young - which rabbits do at that time of the year. They would open up the holes and have the little ones killed because there are too many about. For lots of rabbits are very bad things to get overrun with. They eat corn - yes acres. Where there are plenty they will eat off close for a long way from their burrows. Also I have known in two very sharp winters that the rabbits bit the first year's growth off the hazel and again the next [winter]. Many of the stubs died as the undergrowth was thin. I [recently] looked at the same piece of wood[land]. The young hazel, birch and salix there are now good. So [after] forty years one would not know how it was then. Yet if rabbits are killed as they were, men did not get the chance to snare or get one for themselves, [even] if they were a plague. I have also known of the time when we at home hardly ever had rabbit, but [*sic* - except] when the corn was cut [at] harvest time - unless a chance time I have known father, as I have myself when a lad, pick one up a stoat had killed which only had a little bit eaten just behind Bunny's ears. There were very few around our home. In a meadow where I kept sheep a year or two after I left school there were only two small burrows. This is on Jenkins Farm. Now the gentleman that farms it gives all his men leave to snare them, as did his father years ago. For not many of these Notts care to have rabbits. The men all have certain fields each to snare on. Yet there are [now] always plenty of rabbits when there use to be so few. I know, for a few winters rabbits would fetch 1/6 or 1/9 each. Yet this winter [1936-37] when I caught several, if I sold any I would only get 8d for them. They were not worth the time one has to spend trying to get them, for two or three times I put my ferrets in a rabbit burrow, waited about in the cold an hour before I see one or two come out of the same hole, one stopped in the net. I did not pick up the ferret – I had to wait. Yes I waited for nearly an hour. No more rabbits came out and there were more in that burrow, for I heard them but could not dig for I did not wish to spoil that burrow. In this sandy hill [Brakey Hill] the rabbits has been snared by men who had permission. If so rabbits will often not bolt very freely. That is the place that I [first] ever saw a rabbit caught in a net by ferrets being put in a hole, by a man, [Harry Alston] and his son, who first christened me <u>Tulip</u>.

Control of rabbits

Rabbiting

Brakey Hill

Some notes and conversion tables concerning weights and capacity measures.
The bushel is a capacity measure – it is also the name of the measure used to make the measurement. 1 bushel = 4 pecks (or 8 gallons). 8 bushels of grain were approximately one quarter. 4 bushels = 1 sack or combe. There were regional variations. The following is a general guide from which the estimates on pages 48, 57 & 58 are based. The weight depended upon the produce being measured, e.g.

1 sack of oats	= 12 stone	= 168 lbs (pounds)	or	76.2	kilograms
1 sack of barley	= 16 "	= 224 lbs "	or	97.6	"
1 sack of wheat	= 18 "	= 252 lbs "	or	114.3	"
1 sack of beans or peas	= 14 "	= 266 lbs "	or	120.6	"

Tulip says 'potatoes, turnips, apples, pears etc., were 3 bushel to the sack.' Acorns and stones were also weighed by the bushel. See page 37 for faggot and coal weight.
N.B: lb = a pound weight or 0.4536 kilograms. 14lbs = 1 stone. 112lbs = 1 hundredweight (cwt) or 50.80 Kilograms.
20 cwts = 1 ton. A score is 20.

To the Bird family till sold then it went to the Auberies Estate The Two Cottages were given to the Miss Burkes by their father. The one house next to the one I lived in when I first married. The old Lady lived Rent free. The Rent of the other it was said was used for Charitable uses. Of course I have been told this or I was told by those who perhaps did not Know any More than I do. But was hearsay. Not told by those who Know The Barn was pulled down This was used as a Chaple for Years and I have been to a Service there on Sunday with my parents occasionly. For both my father and Mother attended Church and all of us Bros and two Sisters had to go to Sunday School Then morning and afternoon. Before Church time For all the Time The Rev. C E Raymond was a Parson of Bulmer Church. Church time was Say 1/2 past 10. or eleven oclock in the morning three oclock in Summer. perhaps for a few weeks at 1/2 past two oclock in the afternoons Thus Sunday School was before each Service. Yes Readers the Best too for the Country if only for the Reason that my father Said more than once I know the Rev. Raymond was Parson of the Parish more than 25 years. For when he had been there that time he of times told if he were talking. I have been Clergyman for more than a Quarter of a Centuary he was there a year or two after that but how long I cannot say But there were more folk went to Church also to the Chaple than there are today

Fig 2: Facsimile page from Book 16

It was so hot where the machine was standing under the wind a high hedge very little wind could get Those on the machine put up an awning to keep the sun off. A thather I worked with some years was thatching a big Stack got overpowered by the Sun or heat fell off the ladder on the stack Could do no more that season. The field yielded 10 sacks per acre Not extra but when we cut those peas. There was not a thurtle above the peas neither on the ground could one see a weed of any description unless there was a place the ground was <u>bare</u> Surprising that what land or what one seed can grow — Well I will get to Harvesting operations at Goldingham Hall. When I was 14 & 15- or so yrs old I was Sheep Boy on Jenkins farm I liked the job too for I had a dog who was very fond of me. Those sheep would not get out but little for they knew the dog would soon be after them When I was with them on the Stubbles I had the time of my life plenty nuts to pick two orchards that I could get plenty of apples and some pears I do not think the Master would have said much if he saw us. He might have hallow too at Us Boys but we did not let many see us for we knew times There were some good apples in those orchards too If & The Master had some picked which he did Some times there were put in a Barn with Straw over them. They were quite as good as those in the orchards. We made use of them for the Barn was unlocked in the morning so things were alright for both of us Boys who worked there If one could not go the other could if we

Fig 3: Facsimile page from Book 16

4. THE WEATHER

Heavy Snows

I have read this in a newspaper of an old man being asked by a reporter of a paper, of snows he had known to be deep snows. My uncle Charles Rowe was ten years old [1835] – so this is his version of that one the old man had told [to] the reporter . . . it being put in [the] newspaper that I had read [the] account of. That snow came he said from the south – it blowed off the fields so the roads were full, ditches the same. Rabbits that were in the banks where deep ditches was, did not come out for a long time. [They] moved along the banks under the snow to eat grass etc and did not need to come out. At such places the hedges were so laden with snow where the wind could not blow [it] off, [that] small pieces of wood were buried in the ditches, broken, splintered or bent down so as to fill up the ditch and did not rise when the snow melted, but kept [there] till it were cut down at a future time. The fields being small the snow did not melt on the north side of hedges so that many lands could not be sown with spring corn. Headlands are four yards wide, the plough-horses turning in this place with plough, drill, harrow, roll etc. These four yards are plowed and sown either before or after when the field is drilled with corn therein. Many fields were thus not sown that year or season, as it was covered with snow till late spring. I do not doubt this of what was told me, for my uncle did not tell me a tale that was wrong.

1835

Rabbits in banks

Snow lays until late Spring

As I have mentioned one deep snow that came with a strong wind, perhaps it will be as well to write of another dreadful day much worse, for on the 18th January 1881[i] a blizzard swept over East Anglia, if not all over England. I was ten years old [the] next day, [the] 19th inst. I went to school – how bitter it was when I went down the school meadow. I well remember we children kept looking out of the windows to see a very fine snow falling fast for an hour or more. I do not know what time the snow come on thick. We used to take our dinners to school and eat it before the fire in the old schoolroom – the new school being added onto when I was a few years old, two or three I think.[ii] There were a lot of children that went to school then from nearly all over the parish. Very few, only those whose parents were better off, went to the British School[iii] then – stewards and policemen's children etc.

Blizzard 18th January 1881

Bulmer School

The British School, Sudbury

One of my school pals [Jim][iv] who was about a year older than me, lived with an aunt of his who was my father's first cousin, [as was] his mother also. He was a

---

[i] in the original Tulip says 1888 – this must be a mistake in this instance because he was ten years old, but there was evidently some confusion between the snow stories.

[ii] Extension of the 1870s - See *Bulmer Then and Now*, page 34.

[iii] Mill Lane, Sudbury, erected 1846. *History of Sudbury Suffolk*, Grimwood and Kay, 1952.

[iv] He 'at school was subject to fits. These he had often at times. As he grew older they wore off him, but at times he could get little work to do. Then he would be morose. He was a very funny one to work with unless he took to [someone and then] they [could do] nothing wrong. [For] should anyone say anything against such a one he would flare out – did not forgive or forget for a long time [even] if for a leg pull or fun' – Tulip: Book 16 page 15.

big lad just as big for his age as me were little. Anyhow we would be together if possible, for I suppose [if] he could think of no mischief [then] I could – that was the reason I take it. When we children left school that night or afternoon he said to me "I will go with you a little way down the lane [Green Lane] tonight." We did [so] to about halfway to my home when we came to a tree that was broken off below the branches leaving a long stump standing. We found a big piece that was broken off for the fire – if he could take [*sic* - manage] it. He started off with it against the wind. So I told him I would help him to the wide part of the lane nearer to his home. When I got there I retraced back. What a walk! One could not see far ahead back to the wind. If one faced it one could not get their breath – had to hang [one's] head down or side-face [it]. The snow was as fine as dust and very thickly it fell. I got home alright. Mother asked where my sister was. I did not know but that she went off with the other children round the Street way – which is further but usually better walking, as the lane had cart tracks. Also if horses or cows were drove up, it was not good walking unless fine weather and dry. Mother gave me something to take for my sister to put over her head to keep the snow off. When I got about one third of the way to the street I met the other party. I think there were some grownup person – a woman who had some children – to meet them. So things were alright so far, but I got wrong for coming on home alone, but what for I do not know.

Lane to Upper Houses

Well we lived only one mile or thereabouts from school and had the wind at our back. But what about the children who had to go to the group of some twenty or more houses that had children to go to Bulmer School?[i] For it was near two miles as could be and head wind all the way. It must have been a terrible journey for the big ones let alone the little dears who used to go to school at that time, for all my brothers went to school soon after they were three years old. Of course some of them had a parent to come – some had not. But no doubt they kept together. But I can picture what it was [like] that night, for these are large fields that the wind swept the snow from into the Low Road under the lee a bit. The road was full of snow and if a gateway was leading into the road or a large gap [with] no hedge, the snowed poured off the field as no one can tell but those that have seen such as they could that night. Me and my mate, Jim, when we went down that lane [saw] at a gateway off that large field [where] the snow was up in a heap as high as I were, if not higher. It was said one little girl floundered into the snow into a ditch.

Batt Hall

3-year-old schoolchildren

My! When I got home our house had the full force of the wind, being full west in a hill. Through a misfit of the front door of our house there was a trail of snow right across the house where the snow came through the crack. The wind roared in our large chimney – we thinking the top bricks would come down as had been known at times, for this one is very high.

Snow in house

Well this day was a Tuesday – was called for many years Black Tuesday. When I did go to Sudbury, which was not long after I know, [I saw] what havoc the wind did – also the snow. Great limbs were broken by force of wind and weight of snow [from a] large cedar tree at a house of the same name,[ii] also some large ones [of] the same kind at the Auberies.

---

[i] Tulip most likely had Batt Hall in mind.
[ii] The Cedars –now Dower House - Bulmer Street.

24

Although not alive now – or his wife perhaps – a son of the Rev. O.E. Raymond, named Philip was married to a Miss Fisher of Liston - adjoining Foxearth near Long Melford. The wedding party was at his grandfather's Rectory of Middleton, near Sudbury. They were drove in a cab. This cab and the horse overturned in a lake in the Rectory grounds through losing the road. What a day it was to be sure, a lot of wind and fine snow, as fine as dust. No place was free from snow that day inside or out. If it came through a keyhole it made a fine white mark across the house. The 1st March was another such day, but the snow was not so fine. The snowy Tuesday it drifted more and there was some snow lying about the north side of some hedges in a ditch till Easter time, when we children went to gather primroses for Easter decorations for the church. If we took the flowers to the Rectory we all had a bun or cake, which was a treat to most of us village children. But that year primroses were very scarce.

Wedding carriage overturns

I have known another Easter since when there were as few. It was 1887. That year the day before good Friday two young ladies were driven by two men from Sudbury, [they] came to Goldingham Hall Wood to find primroses and they could find but very few. The winter was not gone, for the dunghill I was helping to get away for the mangolds was froze in the north side of the hill a yard in. When Good Friday was that year I cannot say, but one could know if one looked in an old Prayer book of the Church of England.

Sudbury folk come to gather primroses

The earliest deep snow that I have known happened on Thursday 27th November 1889[i] – Sudbury Market day. A butcher who lived at Cross Street, Sudbury – A. Spring by name – broke his leg through slipping down on his way to market.

Perhaps the severity of another heavy snowfall on the first of March 1886 made such an impression on Tulip that he remembers some work on which he was engaged at the beginning of the fall. It might also add a little light relief to some otherwise serious occasions. Some of the early detail has been omitted.

About the first of March 1886, my uncle [Charles] heard of an old thatched cottage that stood in the hollow between the gate leading to the Auberies garden and the Lodge Gate and House - [beside] the icehouse - where my cousin George [and uncle Charles lived, was to be demolished]. He went to see Colonel Burke and it was sold to him for £5, to be pulled down and all material cleared away. My uncle, knowing that fresh work of any kind interested me, went to where I was working asking the farmer, Mr. Payne of Clapp's farm, to let me come and help pull the old house down. I believe the old chap would have liked not to spare me, but my uncle promised him not to keep me, only for pulling down the old house. It was arranged for me to be there on Monday at six o'clock in the morning. It still snowed, as it had when I came first, but much faster. The wind was in the east. Where we were was the west side of a plantation. We could hear the wind but not feel much of it for it was a large thick wood or plantation, so we were under the wind a lot as was the house to be pulled down. Sometime after, perhaps ten o'clock, the carpenters came.[ii] They looked a pretty lot, for they had old coats, sacks, bags or anything they could get to keep off the snow. For where they started from was under the wind – plenty of wind screen for some bit, but when

Old house, bought for £5, to be pulled down in Sandy Lane

Amos family of Little Henny

Bad weather wear!

---

[i] See also 'Rat Money' incident on page 49, which occurred at the same time.
[ii] Men of the Amos family of woodworkers from Little Henny – lead by one Joe Amos - who gave their name to Amos Hill, Little Henny.

they got past the screen into the open that was when they began to feel the effects of a lot of wind with snow. They came principally side-wind, but they had a journey when in the open for about a mile. The master, Joe, when he saw me said, "You [are] here Philip. I am glad, for your uncle has someone to boss him. I cannot [even] if I dare, for he takes no notice of me if I do let out at him. So do you give it to him, for I know he will [do the same to] you if he get the chance". I thought to myself, "I've got a good start [here for] I shall have someone to see fair play if me and uncle fall out". Well the first job they started was to pull the mantle [in effect a chimney] down - a lot of bricks. So there were soon something for me to do. I had to clean the old mortar off the bricks and stack them up. So Joe had to go up the chimney for a bit. He soon let some bricks down. Of course I had a job so I did not look to see every brick he dropped down. But after a time, I hearing a

Joe Amos falls down chimney

bigger noise from where he was working I looked around. There was Joe down in a heap of bricks and soot – he looked a pickle I can tell. Yes, and not a bad word did he say over it either.

That snow was about nine inches or a foot deep and it laid about a fortnight freezing very sharp at night. But when the sun was bright in the daytime one could snowball nicely, for the snow would bind.

Pulling down a chimney

We were not very long in pulling down the house, perhaps a fortnight, for our carpenter friends did not come every day. About a week after, on the Monday, the chimney at the other end was ready to come down. I do not think we had all the house down then, but getting on a lot toward it. This chimney was built up outside the house. It may have touched the house, [but] that is all. Joe said it would do no harm if it were pulled down by a rope. That would not harm the bricks much. "Us party are none too strong," he said "But someone might come along [who might help]," so he fixed a rope ready, trusting for someone to come along. We saw a man coming down the road. My uncle showed him around. He [then] saw another man coming so he made up his mind to ask [him], the shoemaker to help pull on the rope. When the thatcher came in sight, as he knew who it was as soon as he saw him, he asked him. So we all pulled it away from the house - all of us. There might have been about eight of us. We heaved and had to do so again and again. Joe went to look - he loosened a brick or two. We all gave a heave. Down came the chimney. The poor old thatcher in a light suit of some material, fell in all the black slush there were on the garden where he fell. I had to get away for I did not like for him to see me laugh, for he did not feel like that I knew. How the others kept from it I do not know, but they tidied him up a bit and gave him some beer, so he nearly forgot about it when he went away with the shoemaker.

Passers-by persuaded to help

Of Severe Frosts

1890-91 was the sharpest of winters. I know in January 1891 I left the Auberies and Armsey farms. Soon after I came away I went to two men who were filling up a disused earth pit that clay had been carted from to make bricks etc. The frost was in the land that had to be put in [to fill the pit]. The pit was frozen so thick that when the thaw came the undermined sides of the pit [caved in]. I think there were three heavy falls of snow in the 1890-91 winter.

The next bad winter I have known was 1895 or 1896. I think the first but [am] not sure – one of the two. In the months of January and first week in February of that year whichever it is. I know of a case that happened at Borley in a deep snow. One morning at Borley Place Farm an old school chum of mine who was working on the farm, walked in the snow to a mangold clamp – with straw on top to prevent the frost from harming the mangolds – to see if there were a rabbit under the straw. He was surprised to see a footprint of feet without shoes on. He followed those tracks to an old shed in a meadow – [it was] used for colts to keep away from flies etc in summer and in winter to feed the same if put in [the] meadow. He found a poor man there exhausted by the cold – his feet were frozen. He ran to his master – told him. He sent for a doctor and [the man] was sent to Sudbury Union where the poor man had to have his leg amputated. One doctor was Dr. Fletcher, Dr. Mason's assistant, who helped to do the same. Dr. Fletcher somehow got a scratch. Some of the blood from that poor man got into the scratch or so it was said by many – or some folk. That Dr. Fletcher had blood poisoning and was very ill for a long time before he went on duty at Dr. Mason's again. So I take it that frost is bad for human flesh. If it is or not I do not know.[i]

Borley

Man – a tramp? - found in freezing conditions

Sudbury Union and leg amputation

This frost started a few days before February 8th. How long I cannot say, but there were that year weeks and weeks of frost very sharp. Ice was the thickest on ponds that I ever [did] see. We could get no potatoes out of the clamps – it was so hard. If we had broken the earth to get some out we could not have kept the frost out. We borrowed a bushel or more from one of my workmates as he had a spare room in an old house next to his that was thatched. He said they were not froze. They did not seem to be and they were good, but after the thaw the few we had [left] of them told the tale, for they were very wet and not good – for they were frosted. No one can cover a clamp up well after a frost has set in so sharp, unless they can get a lot of straw etc. What a time it was for all wild things. Birds, especially blackbirds and thrushes were starved to death. Plenty were seen in holes under stumps where the poor things got to find shelter and died. There was a very large flock of wild pigeon around our part. In two or three days they got so poor they were all skin and bone. I was told by those who used to shoot them in the woods [that] they were not worth a cartridge. They used to come on our allotments after a bit of green and one used to come into the gardens. I borrowed a gun, shot at it – but did not kill it. It flew to a tree about a quarter of a mile [away]. Next morning it laid there and the rooks were around it and picked what little meat they could off it. Rooks picked turnips, swedes and anything that came their way. They got onto corn stacks and pulled corn out where they could.

Thick ice

Hungry birds

The frost was in the ground till late March. I know it was a time for blue beans that father used to grow for soup. So one day I thought I would dig a piece of land for them. I went on the allotment and dug up a bit where we had our potatoes the season before. The frost was not out of the ground as deep as the spade was and all the potatoes I found were soft. I could squeeze the water out of them. I sowed the peas but did not dig any more of the potato ground for some time, but when I did I found several potatoes good – so the frost had got out of them, for plenty were not in the ground more than three inches. The frost on the level was a yard I should think.

Frost a yard deep

---

[i] Tulip's father, David, lost a finger as a result of a thorn puncture causing blood poisoning; dated elsewhere as 1894 or 1895. In a similar happening his uncle lost a hand. When writing of this Tulip says, 'When these calamities happened there were a white frost both times. Is frost a poison to one's flesh?'

Frozen barges on the River Stour

The six or seven, perhaps more, bargemen who navigated the Stour for Mr. R.A. Allen and Sons – who the barges belonged to – could not get their barges away from various places up and down the river for many weeks. They had very little food, neither had they but little money. The brickyard workers, carpenters and bricklayers about Sudbury, if alive could tell a tale of that winter much better than I can now though I saw a lot myself as I will presently [tell].

Brundon Hall

A Mr. Whittome, a gentleman who farmed Brundon Hall of over five hundred acres, growed a great many acres [of potatoes]. One year he planted seventy acres or more. Whether it was the time of this frost I cannot say. Anyhow he had long clamps of potatoes about the farm. How many clamps I cannot say. These clamps had a lot of farmyard manure over the earth that was put on to protect from frost. This outer covering was pushed to one side by some folks from the town – night or morning – when it was dark or [there were] not many [about] to see what they were doing. Yes this gentleman had tons and tons it was said taken from the clamps. When the thaw came along the clamps fell down and was out of order. The potatoes being taken away when the frost got out of the earth [the clamps] gave way [and] so it caved in where the potatoes should have been. Of course he had the Sudbury police at the scene but the potatoes were not there, neither were the folk that took them. It was said that the potatoes walked across the common over the Stour. Yes it could bear the ice, for I saw ice on the river as thick as [from] my fingers to my elbow.

Deep ice on river

Sometimes I had been to St. Leonard's Hospital on a Sunday to see [my father] there – for I used to go most Sundays and he was there for weeks at that time.[i] So I used to walk along the river to Brundon and get to Bulmer that way. Not a great distance farther [*sic*] – perhaps a mile. Along the river there were a wide crack – inches wide perhaps – that did not freeze. That is where I put my arm down to find the thickness of the ice. From that crack the ice fell to the bank. The ice was higher in the middle. My father told me that when he was a convalescent in hospital and were allowed to go for walks or down the town, men were digging across Sudbury Market Hill to find the water pipes that had bursted through the frost. They were down as deep as he were high – 5ft 10ins or 5ft 11ins. The pipes down [there] were full of ice. "Did it freeze from the top?" I asked. "No, I should say through." So many bursted that water had to be taken around by carts and folks had to pay so much per pail. Also a soup kitchen was opened.

Pipes frozen 5' down on Sudbury Market Hill

Soup kitchen

My poor mother was laid up with rheumatic fever. My younger brother [James] was a little over a year old – poor me had to wean him. I know well enough but he forget I will be bound. I was nurse, housekeeper and manager till my sister [Agnes] could get home from Dullingham. I think she could not get home for a week or so but she came as soon as possible – when she did get home there was plenty for her to do. But we got through alright. I went to work in a wood when I could. It was piecework so it made little difference, for that I did not do my mates did and had the money for what they did.

Tulip's sister Agnes

The following incident is not dated.

---

[i] After David Rowe's finger amputation above.

It is surprising how far frost will find water. I know that me and my son, Tom, was told to go to Rookery Farm, Acton, near Long Melford. When we got there we were to tie straw in bundles to put on the railway to [be transported to] where [it was] wanted.[i] This wheat-straw stack was not thatched. When I got to the top of the stack [I saw it was] very wet as it was rather flat, so the water did not run off but soaked down the stack in what we call pipes. This wet straw was frozen so tight that I could not do anything in the way of pulling all the wet [stuff] off till I got to [the] dry I was to tie for sale. So I went to see that farmer who it belonged to – asked him if he would send a man or two with a cart and horses or a wagon to put the wet frozen straw on to, so as the wet straw should not be in our way in the tying of bundles. He told two men to come down to the stack for they both had a horse and cart each. They were soon there so that we three or four between us loosed [sic] some of the top wet. Of course if one big lump of straw was taken off perhaps there were a piece that was dry so no frost would stick. We cleared enough for me to make a start for I did not mind a little wet, for we can work a little wet in with plenty of dry straw. This straw was [of] the hardest, straightest, brittlest [type of] straw. This was sown in the early spring – a kind of wheat suited to grow February or early March. We could not make bands [or withes] with it but had to go to the farm a little distance away. We were not long in tying this stack – a week perhaps, maybe more. When in the centre or halfway down where the water had worked down [the] pipes it was frozen – [at] least it was three yards from the sides. This was so right down to the bottom – icy straw.

Rookery Farm Acton

Frozen straw

Severe Hail Storm – 1897

I will get to the storms that swept a large part of Bulmer two times since I have been married. The first of the two I was cutting at Ballingdon in a three-acre meadow in June 1897. It was a Thursday. Hot, it was hot. There was not a leaf that stirred. We had some beer – that was needed. It was so hot we drank all we had [and then] wanted another drink. It was too hot for us to work. One of us took the bottle to the pub near and had it filled. Then we had a rest – might as well. Too hot for cutting that long grass. No sun was to be seen for hours that day. How long we rested I do not know. The work we did hardly paid for our drinks. We went home at night-time and next day we heard that a dreadful thunderstorm around Chelmsford had played havoc - glass broken by hail in the many glasshouses of the market gardeners etc. So bad it were that a few of the poor men who thought nothing but of their ruin, done away with themselves. A sorry plight but very hard on those who belonged to them – their wives and children. What a thing [that] one of nature's freaks should turn men or women to such extremities, for that no one can possibly help. This Reader was about twenty-five miles from Sudbury. Yet the heat was so oppressive.

Cutting hay at Ballingdon

Dreadful storm near Chelmsford

Suicides

Of the other storm, this happened a month later in Bulmer. This was also on a Thursday. A hot day too, but not so dull or so hot for so long or I did not notice it. That particular day the Whitely men, who were working on the House [Goldingham Hall] had in the dinner hour a game of boxing between a village man of about my age and [one of their men]. The match occurred at the Hall. It was made out at the dinnertime to put up a ring and they were to fight each other with gloves on. A rope and stakes were put up and a ring formed. The steward and

Goldingham Hall

The Great Boxing Match

---

[i] Note brevity of the original dialect version – "put on the railway to where wanted".

others [were] to see this Great Boxing Match. Of course it just pleased these Cockneys. The one they put him [i.e. the village man] onto was a boxer from London – [he] of course kept it up being pleased for a break and to see this man up against him so. That Arthur, [the Cockney,] would be sure to win. Bets were made and all were in order for the fight. I did not go home for dinner that day [but stayed] to see the fun. I told the wife that I should not come today so the food was not to be cleared away. The fun started. It was worth seeing of course. No one was hurt, but Arthur got very angry over it. But by that time the sun was covered up by a cloud as if a storm was brewing up. And so it did before many were ready for it, as it came on so quickly. Yes it was a storm. Hail fell there very thickly – some hail were as big as walnuts. When it was over how cold it turned – one wanted a coat on. I kept about till it was time to go home. There were four or five of us walked up the drive to the road. I did not go the nearest [way] as I had someone to go with, as they [the men] were in different places on the farm at work till the storm drove them to shelter [there was] plenty to talk [about] of the storm.

Hail as big as walnuts

I had my supper and went up the field between my house [at Lower Houses][i] and the Upper Houses where father lived. This field, [Upper Fields & Nonsuch,] is fairly steep before the Upper Houses are reached, so one can hardly see the large chimney till going up the hill for a bit, or it used to be so. I know now the hill is not so steep as it were fifty years ago as the land was worked down off the crown of the hill. When I got to the top of the hill hail stones laid much thicker – [it was] white with the icy hail. I was surprised to see this when I got home or [more correctly] at my father's. What a sight! The upstair windows were broken. A heap of hail, three or four barrow-fulls, were taken from out of my father's pig court. I went down the garden. It was enough to make one cry. In that garden not a whole leaf could be seen. On rhubarb of the giant kind – great stalks with leaves as big as umbrellas – not a particle of leaf only ribs. French beans, or runners, just on bloom were the same - also a bed of broccoli plants [of] a late kind ready to be planted out, [as it was] then early enough to get some good ones in late May or June. I never saw such a sight.

Top of hill ploughed off

Windows broken at Upper Houses

I soon went to my own home. It was much worse. Nearer to the barn there were loads of hail that were washed from a cartway into a meadow. At the barn, where the hail had come off the barn there were [still] hail on the Tuesday morning. My father who was an auxiliary postman did a round every day. The post round was to the Brick Yard and the one or two cottages around and then to Butlers. There were no hailstones near there. They did not hardly believe it had been so bad. Father took them the hail on Tuesday morning and it was summer time. Of course the hail was on the north side of the barn – no doubt where the sun had little power in the shade of a tree or two near. The little two-and-a-half acre field [Osborns or Osbeans] of barley between the barn and my field, when this were threshed there were little corn, for the hail had knocked off the barley ears. A twelve-acre field of mangolds caught it well – there were not a whole leaf in the field. Also the bark on wood of oak and hazel caught the full force of hail. Bits as big as sixpences [had] bared [parts of the bark of hazel] white and for some years after where [this] hazel was hit by the hail and the bark was bruised, no withes could one wind. Hedge nuts were then nearly full size. If hail hit a nut, which then is soft, that part bruised. When ripe the dent was in the kernel of that nut, for on

Very localised – none at Butler's Hall

Crops ruined

Hazel nuts bruised

---

[i] Tulip started his married life at Lower Houses, but later moved to Upper Houses.

this black spot it did not grow. Three times a reaper had to cut round a twenty-seven acre field of oats at Goldingham Hall. First a scythe had cut around and [all the sheaves were] tied. Of the standing crop half the oats [had been] hailed off. On another farm, The Hill Farm, Gestingthorpe, seven acres were spoiled of oats. This was insured against hail.

Hail Storm, July 1912

One Saturday in July 1912, The Friendly Society of Girls were having a treat. These treats were held at various Rectories in the district. Farmers lent their wagons for the occasion. The Bulmer girls were going, as others were at the same time, to meet at Borley Rectory, which is near the church. The churchyard has some of the best-kept yew trees or shrubs – there are few kept better. There was a terrible storm overtook the parties as they were going through Bulmer and up the road to Borley Church. I did not see but heard of it by letter and also by a man who was working [in] that part of Smeetham Hall. He told me it was an ice storm. He saw ice – jagged bits – half as big as his hand. [The part of] this field of wheat [where the man was working] had the worst of the storm – was cut about ever so. The water rushed down this long field, more I [would] say than half a mile down the hill to the road, which is flat to the bridge forty or fifty yards away. The road had silt or earthy mud to the depth of 2ft or 1 ½ ft, so a motor that tried to get through got stranded. My brother, George, was a partner of a threshing set with a Borley man named F. Scrivener.[i] They had the threshing of the [damaged] wheat. There were very few sacks per acre, which, if it had not been hailed [on would] maybe come upward to ten sacks per acre. Two or three fields of corn at Smeetham Hall also caught the brunt of the storm. The Friendly Girls – those caught in the storm – all had to change their <u>Clothes</u>.

Girls Friendly Society outing

Borley Rectory

Bardfield bridge

Severe Rain Storm

The Sunday before August Bank Holiday one of the years of the War [1914-18] there was a terrific thunder storm. It rained in torrents. I was indoors, but it was said by those that were out it was a cloud burst. My donkey was tied up out in the lane – up by where I lived [Upper Houses]. When it was over I went to see after it and get it home. The water was rushing down the road like a river. My wife and lads had gone to chapel. After I got the donkey in the stable I went down the road to what is called The Runlet – a culvert - runs under the road here. When I got there I could not go through, as there was so much water. I went and put the donkey in the cart and thought I would [then] go through. [When] I got back there was a bigger flood. It was no use for me to think of it. I [either] tied my donkey up or took it back – I am not sure which. I was there when the chapel folk came to the water. I got through the hedge some bit up the road and went across a gateway leading to another field. The water was rushing over the gateway. I rolled my trousers up and waded through – it was up to my knees. I had hard work to keep on my legs but I got through alright, up the fence a little way and got over and walked across a field of barley to the road where my wife and boys and some of my neighbours were standing. A poor old lady had a son at home ill. She was in a way [*sic* - a state of agitation] to get home to him, but I would not let her go as she said she would. I told her John would be alright, as the water would go down as

Floods across road to Upper Houses

---

[i] Tulip says that Scivener 'died through sceptic [*sic*] in Colchester Hospital after his arm was very much damaged in a chaff cutting machine'. Tulip: Book 16 page 58.

fast as it rose when the bulk of water had passed through and it was not cold and would not be dark for a long time. A brother of mine who lived at Wickham St. Paul's came to see his wife's people [and so] he thought he would come and see the water as he knew there would be likely to be a flood after such a storm. He got by one lot of water that was deep in the road, by getting over the hedge as the others had done that had got to The Runlet. He saw what a plight they were in. He went back, put his pony in the cart and drove through the water. It flowed so strong that it swayed the cart on one side although it was loaded. The fear I saw was if the water burst the welham,[i] as some calls it. [Later] they had a change [of clothes] and we had tea.

Bulmer Tye

Afterwards my father and me made up our minds to go on the Tye, which us did. What a mess there was. A [deep] ditch – so one could not see out of it – did not carry the water, it washed over the field. Some clover looked as if rolled. Also on the way [there] some buckwheat were the same. On Bulmer Tye near The Fox it had looked like a wide river – the grass was covered with mud. There was a mess of mud and water. We got home just before dusk. How slippery it was. Slosh, slosh, - very bad walking.

Repairing storm damaged roads

Next day in the road that goes past our cottages it was all ruts in some parts – the stone was washed off. I went and got the surveyor. He asked me if I could do something, with my two sons, to help rectify [it] so traffic could get on. I said I could for a day or two. So he left the road that goes my way to me as he had a lot of other parts to go and see what damage was done through the storm. I used my donkey cart to cart the metal back in. The holes in the road near The Runlet was covered with mud inches deep and it stuck like pitch as there was not much grit in it to clean off the shovel. One of my sons went to help on the Gestingthorpe Road with another old chap. The Watery Road [or Gestingthorpe Road, passing through Lower Houses] was in a terrible state. A man was seeing after sheep near and had a pony cart to ride back and to the sheep. He started to go home as soon as the storm was over. He stood up in the cart – it washed his buckskins out and nearly upset the pony and cart. The volume of water came on more after he got to the narrow way. It washed oat sheaves out of one field into another and took all the soil off a headland. [In a] field which was sown with red mangolds it washed some away. On the subsoil you could see the mangold roots as fine as spider webs all over the ground. It washed a stile up near the allotment field, which I straightened up a time after. It washed potatoes up in the gardens and in the cottage I was married into, the water was up to the chair seats and the garden – for the man took a lot of trouble [with it] – was all mud and looked desolate. In the next field [Dysters or thereabouts] the soil was washed off several rods. I went and looked over it. I kicked the bone handle of a budding knife, the blade was rusted and one could have picked [up] dozens of old nails, such it was at that time about this part. Half a mile away due south there stands a clump of Scots fir trees [Deal Nursery] The field that joins it is Combes Hill – twenty-four acres or so with heavy and light soils in it. Some parts are very sandy and part level. The southern part slopes to south. What a mess that was. In this corner ditches filled with sand drift. Hundreds, I should think, of tons. Furrows were knee deep and at the top a yard wide or more. The ditch had not been opened out last year [1926] at this time.

Beside lane to the Brickyards

---

[i] A local dialect word - usually spelt 'wellum' - is a brick built culvert under a road or field gateway, not just a pipe or little bridge. See *An Essex and Suffolk Alphabet,* by Basil Slaughter.

Memories of heavy rainfalls – all three connected to weddings

In 1907 Miss Nora Burke, of The Auberies, was married to a Mr Braithwaite. Tulip, his brother Sid and a Johnny Rash got leave from their master – no name given – to attend the wedding [i.e. observe from outside the church] and an unexpected 2/6 to drink the bride's health.

. . . . at what time it began to rain I cannot say, but it more than rained, it poured down fast. We what went to the wedding were near the church – for us three did not go in – had to have something on that the water ran off or they would be soaking wet, their clothes anyway. It spoiled the day. Anyway they managed to get an awning for the bride to walk under from the end of what we children called the coach road across the school meadow; for that used to be wide enough for a vehicle to go across without the wheels touching the grass. Now I see it is only a path four feet or so [wide]. Well there were four of us who went to see that occasion. After it were over we took ourselves to the Fox Inn to drink the bride and bridegroom's health.

Another wet wedding on Saturday May 7th 1889, although not attended by Tulip, remained in his memory. Of the day he says . . .

My! How it rained on that day [starting] early in the morning, so neither of us[i] went to work. We laid our hoes in a ditch that parted two fields without a hedge – just green banks. This field was in Middleton parish, near a mile from the farm. On Sunday 8th May there was such a flood at Sudbury, so a boat was out in Ballingdon Street. Folks who attended the churches and chapels etc., when they went that day had to be conveyed through the water by conveyances. Some were carts etc., for Ballingdon was then in Essex. Now it is in the Borough of Sudbury, that is in Suffolk.[ii]

Tulip's own wedding did not escape a severe downpour. At the time of the wedding he was living in one of a pair of cottages at Lower Houses [see Map1 opposite Page1]

. . . the first [cottage] from The Street and it was where we kept our wedding up. There were about thirty friends and relatives of both sides. I was married on the Monday after Xmas 1896. What a wet day it was. I had to run like hunting to the church [interesting phrase] or I should have been wet through.[iii] My coat was not very dry as it was. After describing the festivities he continues . . . we broke up about midnight. A man from the Inn was ordered to be there at twelve o'clock with a conveyance to take my wife's mother, sister and brother home, which was about two miles off, on Finch Hill. When the man came to the door to say he was ready we packed them off. But what a night. The water was rushing under the bridge [over a ditch between the road and the house] touching the bearers and a very big flood there was in the town the next day.

---

[i] He had been working on fields at Armsey Farm with his uncle Charles and another young man.
[ii] Transferred from the administrative county of Essex to that of West Suffolk in September 1896.
[iii] The distance from house to church is about three-quarters of a mile.

Severe Winds

*Bulmer School-
Tulip allowed out
of school to look
after a brother!*

I will now mention of a very high wind that blowed all day one Friday in October, [1881] but I do not know what day of the month, neither have I ever heard since when the date of the day was, or I would be able to tell – for I seldom forget for all time if I make up my mind to remember anything. I know I went to school and sometime in the morning my mother came to school and brought my little brother Charlie. She brought him with her so she could go out and pick acorns. The Governess let me go to look after my young brother. The governess let me look after him. It was a dry day one may be sure. I got out into the school meadow and into the churchyard. There is a short avenue of lime trees [with] two horse-chestnut trees on the left side of the gate and two to finish the avenue, one each side of the church porch. One grew large chestnuts. They were tumbling down. We soon filled our pockets with them. Then we thought of the sweet chestnuts that growed in a plantation.[i] We emptied our pockets, for my little brother had a pocket, although it was in his pinafore. Away we went. Sweet chestnuts do not ripen so early as the horse chestnut. We did not find very many, only on the largest tree did they fall off. When we found all we could we got into the road. In the meadow on the other side [were] a lot of walnut trees – five or six large ones.

*Scrumping
walnuts*

"Come on Charlie," I said, "and I will see if there are a few walnuts down." So I turned into a field just above the meadow and keeping my eyes open to see [*sic - find*] a place where I could get through. I did not till halfway along. [There was] no gap but there the fence or hedge was elm [with] no prickles on. I got through for I was not afraid of wood. Thorns are quite another thing, not only do they prick but will make a hole in your clothes. Not so with elm or other wood. I told Charlie to stop and I would bring some walnuts for him. I hustled around. There were a nice lot, which still kept on falling, although not fast. I went around the lot. Not all of them had many on but those that had [were fine]. I thought I had better have another look before I left. That was where Tulip made a blunder. He ought to have been satisfied with those he had got, for on the second round someone was coming. I knew well who it was too. I started to run. Then knowing Charlie was over in the field and that I could not leave him there I had to stand my ground. I did not try to run away. When he came up to me [he said], "Oh, it is you Philip. You have no business here after my walnuts. How many have you got?" He knelt down beside me to see. I emptied my pockets wondering all the time what he was going to do to me. Of course I had to cry. It was all I could do. But I told him, or [so he told] old Harry Alston afterwards, [that] I should not have been there had I known that he was coming. "I know," he said ""I do not suppose you would." He let me go at that. But I heard of that [incident] from old Harry Alston for years, yes and years after. You may be sure it was a case of, 'be ye sure your sins will find you out.' I know he did not forget to let me know. [The gentleman], Mr. John Parmenter English let me have the walnuts.

Tulip continues his narrative of that day's winds

Oaks uprooted

Well what a day for wind. There were some windfall branches we used to get for the fire, for nothing was said of picking up a bough from trees what the wind blew off. But this wind did more than that. It uprooted oaks and large ones at that – I

---

[i] Further along Church Road, towards Bulmer Street.

34

know it is not often one find an oak uprooted. But it twisted large boughs or arms of oak as large as my thigh is now, or more. I would show a person one of them were I near. Also an oak top that was twisted and broken about so that the whole top was cut off near the trunk. That oak I have watched grow ever since and to look at from the ground the limbs or branches look not bigger than a man's thigh at present – although if cut off they would look much bigger.

Near the Brick Yard, by the sandpit on the Hedingham Road, there were a lot of high poplar trees belonging to or part of the Butlers Farm or Hall. On some of them mistletoe grew. These trees were uprooted – nearly all of them anyway. Only one poplar left standing now on the same ground. I say standing if so called – the proper thing to say of it is leaning, for when I was against this tree a few weeks ago [I noticed] this tree leaned from the ground toward the east as all poplars do. It surprised me that it could lean so much without having the west side root up or break off - for there must be tons of the bole or trunk without taking into consideration the weight of the limbs and branches of the big top. For [poplar] is a very heavy wood when green, especially when the leaves are on – also at other times. Yet when seasoned it is one of the lightest of woods. Largely used for the making of wood shovels for the throwing of corn in barns when dressing for market. Also for the making of mud scoops for the use of throwing mud from ponds or rivers. Also this wood has been used a lot for building purposes – as rafters and studs in the building of cottages. Those other trees were all uprooted by that wind. Although I did not see them, many of them were partly across the road so that no vehicle could pass. That is one instance of what the high wind did. I knew of another long line of trees in a neighbouring parish, Great Henny, standing beside the river or fairly near, that one could see from the road. That row was uprooted one after the other as if put down by man at a given time with roots standing up leaving a big hole. One can see [that] when one gave way through [the] force [of the wind] it helped uplift the roots of its neighbour [and] so with the others that all came down.

When I was attending sheep for Mr. D. Gardiner in a field not far from Great Henny church I went into a small grove where [some poplars grew]. Two poplars that were not far apart had been blown down by this high wind in October. The old roots were there where the tree had been sawn off and taken away. The holes that were made by those two falling poplars was as if to say a square rod of land had been set up on end. Say a yard or more thick. It was about four years after this strong gale.

Enough of trees. Stacks and [more] stacks had all their tops blown off, both round and square or oblong – which you will. Tiles, slates and thatch from off houses, barns and cottages everywhere around. That terrible gale that blowed practically all day on that Friday was called for years [after] 'That Windy Friday.'

Hedingham Road poplars and mistletoe

Damage by more fallen poplars at Great Henny

Uses of poplar

Great Henny

Row of trees uprooted – domino effect!

Damage by more fallen poplars at Great Henny

Damage to corn stacks and buildings

Back row standing from left to right – Philip ('Tulip', b1871),
Charles (b1879) Agnes (b1872), Harry (b 1877), Albert (b1882)

Seated – David (father, b1842), Eliza (mother – nee Finch b1847),
Sidney (b1884)

Standing between parents – James (b1894)

Front – seated on floor – George (b1888), Emily (b1890)

Fig 4: David & Eliza Rowe with sons and daughters c1896
(probably taken at time of Tulip's wedding)

5. WOODLAND CRAFT

The length of this chapter may not do justice to the amount of time that Tulip must have spent engaged upon woodland work, for a considerable amount of anecdotal content is included - e.g. the loss of an arm and finger by his uncle and father and reflections on the 'Champion Hedger'. However many references can be found dotted about the writings wherever mention is made of the uses of woodsmen's tools and timbers.

Hedging

There is a lot of difference in cutting one hedge down to another in many ways. For I have cut hedges that are many years in growth. One hedge I done once, with help sometimes, had not been cut as long as many could remember. In that case one would have to use an axe - if the stuff is large a billhook is not the thing [to use]. Although I should not perhaps take an axe for a few pieces, as they [axes] are no better for lying about [even] if one is sure no one would take it away - but these are not so likely to be taken by daylight. As for a billhook, that, one can put away in a pocket. Sometimes a fence is a boundary fence near a meadow that is fed by cattle. Such hedges have to have a thick high hedge put on if the ditch is to be cleaned out and the bank rectified, as is often the case. Of course nowadays barbed wire is used to stop gaps in hedges where cattle feed, but there was not much or any used at one time. Bad stuff it is too to work near for it hooks anything. The best way is to get it out of the way first, for it is dangerous to a tool and one cannot swing an axe handy where it is.

Tools

At some farms men used to cut hedges at so much per rod to cut the hedge off and do the ditch. Then so much per score for bush or wood faggots. The round wood or batlings were so much per heap of a certain size. Some men were satisfied with fences done that way. They would keep busy winding the withes in their dinnertime. So if a man went home to meals and worked as hard, he did not make the time up according to [*sic* - in the opinion of] the other man if they were both good at it. I have known men go into a wood to tie small faggots - these were what is called tits.[i] They had 6d per score and could tie up one hundred per day. Some that went to the same job could only tie sixty tits. The faggots that was usually tied up in our part would average about 70lbs or the weight of a bushel of coal - as this is how coal used to be sold. I have, and so have [many] more men, pitched them on a cart alone, but it was too much really for one. It was much better if two did it for they could lay them on the cart better. It is not a nice job to move a faggot of that size [and put it on other faggots] for they are not nice things to walk on as one can slip between them easy. Faggots at that size were sold at 5/- per score – 3d each. Yet many do not like to pay 6d each now. Then wages was 10/- per week – now 30/-. I have often spoken of it amongst my class. During the last several years [c1927] I have cut a hedge off for wood as I used to when I worked for a master. Then bush faggots were sold at 2/6 per score, now there is no sale for them and we do not bake, so the bushes have to be burned - a slower job than tying them up. On a windy day it will blow the flame through, for if the green wood once get a hold it will burn as fast as one can put it on - but then it wants cutting about.

faggots

Binding faggots

Cost of faggots

---

[i] Small faggots for kindling – EDD.

Uncle loses an arm

Withes [bands] used for tying faggots

Sometimes one could not find withes in a fence, for some kinds of wood will not twist so as to make a band or withe. One kind of elm will not but another kind if it is no bigger than a straw will hold together till it get sear - Maple, ash and a kind of salix [are other] kinds [that] will. Hazel is one of the best - I have seen a great bit wound for a withe especially to put round a scrap faggot - as we used to tie up all sear [or dead wood] and a lot of under-bush for ourselves. That was our perquisite for the use of hook and gloves and [wear] and tear of clothes. For hedging is a rough job whether for wood or bushes. It is not safe to do work without gloves for one is likely to knock skin off their hands - also to get thorns in. But it is not good for gloves when the wood is wet for it spoils them. One can tie wood faggots without if it is not too frosty. To get pricked with a bush when the frost is out is not good for the flesh.[i] An uncle of mine [Charles] was getting some rose buds with roots one very hoary frosty morning about a week into February. He pricked his hand - it turned to blood poisoning. What an arm that was! Swollen up his fingers as big as a fork handle - his wrist as big as his jacket sleeve. The Doctor cut the back of his hand. It laid open as big as a little jointer pig like many that I have helped kill. His arm was swollen up to the shoulder and to see it in bed it looked like a young dressed pig it was so big. He had to go to St. Guy's Hospital. He told me they took the swelling down in a night. He son's and relatives sat up with him. I for one [had] to bathe it with hot fermentations for nine days before he went to London. But he lost his hand and wrist. He lived several years afterwards a nearly helpless cripple, but he could get up and sit outside when the weather was fit. He died at the age of eighty-eight about 1900.

Bushes poisonous in frost.

Blood poisoning

Tulip's father, David, loses a finger

The funny part of it is my father, who was one-armed, [could] cut a hedge off - for the most part blackthorn and wood with plenty of brambles given in. He could do a fence clean and well and tie up faggots as pretty as most people. I know he tied up the best bush faggots that could be tied, for he used to hook them well [and these] were better to put in the oven and also to stack up and to cart. One day the farmer told him he could have a horse and cart to get them home as it was frosty and easy going, for [then] the horse [and cart] did not hurt the land. It was a lovely morning that we, my father and I, got to carting them. It was the 8th February thirty-three or thirty-four years ago [1894 or 1895]. It came on foggy and the bushes got white with frost in a short time. During that time my father said to me, "I have pricked my finger." I had not many more bush faggots to put on the load, for he loaded them - he could do that job best. After we had put a rope over them he got down. Said to me, "See if you can get that bush [*sic* - thorn] out. My finger is painful." He told me where to look but I could not see it. So he put his glove on again for there was a small hole in the forefinger of a nearly new glove. I saw the hole and then I knew where to look for the bush in his finger. But I could not see it. We finished carting all the faggots that was made, for he cleared up close every day he was there as near as he could. I went home with the horse and cart. I knew my father was queer by the look of him and he said his finger was painful. When I

---

[i] See note page 27.

got home, again he said, "You will have to see if you can get that bush out." I was a fairly good hand at taking out thorns and thistles. I had a good knife and it did not hurt me for I did not feel the pain of a burst in one's finger. So folks often gave me a job sometimes I can tell you, when there has been plenty of thistles in the corn we have been tying up. I saw no bush. Next morning he showed it to me again. I said, "I am off to the Doctor's to get him to see it," for I had my doubts although I did not tell father. I started off to town so as to be there at the time to see the Doctor - it was about three miles. The Doctor was up to see him as soon as he could. We were to poultice it with linseed meal, so I had another journey for that. But we had to try bread poultices first. How ill father became. We kept on with the hot poultices [but it got] no better. The Doctor came and he said he would have to go to hospital at once. We got him there. The Doctor looked at it as soon as he was there. Father told me he [the Doctor] looked at his hand and said, "It will have to be cut there and there." Then father said, "You have got it off then," meaning the finger. The Doctor had taken it off at the second joint - without [father] being chloroformed - to save his life. Did he grumble about it? Not he. Two brothers both had blood poison through the same [cause]. One lost part of his arm, the other part of his finger. Both were pricked I believe the same day of the month [8th February] a few years after one another.

No anaesthetics

The Champion Hedger

During the early part of the time the war was on a farm changed hands and had a man [come] to do some hedging in the springtime - for the leaves was on the hedges. He was addressed as the 'Champion Hedger' - a fine name! I know nothing of the man. I have seen him at work and worked with the man he employed to help him. This man told me a lot of him [the Champion Hedger] - as he was told and [what] he saw of the man who called himself thus. Well, the foreman or steward managed the farm, for his master was at the War. Both men I have found as straight as one would wish to meet or work for. And I did a lot one way or another. I used to do thatching and cut hay for the farm. The hay and clover was sold to straw merchants. I also tied straw a lot. I always had one or two of my sons with me unless they were at other work and could not help me - then I would make out as well as I could with help from anyone I could get to help me make bands. I cannot get on well with making bands on my alone [sic], although there are men who can and do make them without help. But I will not for I want and like a mate for such work. Well the foreman thought a lot of this hedger's work. He did it well, but not any better than I could or one or two other men on the farm could have - although not of that pattern for I had not seen any done just like it. I will tell why. He used to nail the biggest pieces down to another growing bit. But had any man around our way had have asked a master for nails, that master would have said, "Withy it down." Another thing, no master would have let his men do hedging at that time of the year, do that farmer is no sportsman - for nearly all the hedging that man did was when the birds was nested. How many keepers or men who think of sport would like to see a man trampling down the nettles and grass etc just as partridges and pheasants are laying their first batch of eggs? It was said he could do a hedge so that a bird could hardly get through. Yes, at that time of year when all wood etc., is in full leaf I could without much ado. This work was done so much per chain. And very good money he did get for it. It was of different prices. I do not know how much, neither did I want to, but I know no farmer would pay so much for hedging around my part - not to their own

Goldingham Hall

The Champion Hedger!

The Champion Hedger's different style

Differential pay for The Champion

workmen. No, nor praise one of them, let alone giving them extra. I went by the man several times. I picked up one of his tools. I told him he had a very narrow edge on them and I had not seen but very few such tools, only a big two-handed one. This tool was called a slasher. A good tool it was which one could use with one hand. But all the time I spoke to the man he always seemed to talk as several people I have had to do with. That is to think we who are native of the parish are very one-eyed and do not know how to do much - [as if to say] "Do the master would not send for me." A man who belongs to my parish as in many more do not boast of that they do - they do it. And in a way it will take the best to beat him in what he can do, for he will do his best. For if there is anything extra to be earned the farmers very often advertise [for outsiders].

I was speaking of thatching stuff - that is long hazel poles. This man did a hedge near a swampy ditch that was too wide to step across. Along this hedge grows hops and other hedge creepers such as bryony, Amaris dulcis [*sic*][i] and wild clematis. The stubs were of elder and salix [willow] for the most part. The hedge was treated in this Champion's style. How? There had to be cut out of the wood long bits of wood, hornbeam, hazel and other bits that could be mauled about by 2inch wire nails to stop the cattle, for this hedge is between the low meadows and the large field of forty-three acres or more - a very hilly field too. A lot of the [bits] put along this fence were useful - what would have been good poles in a year or two. This fence had been done times before. No cattle could go over if a fair hedge was put on after the hedge was cut off. Why? Because the people who farmed the land before used to have this wide ditch cleaned out now and again. No cattle will or can jump over a wide ditch that is soft near, as that hedge is. When that had been cleaned out, the next spring it was full of watercress. A lovely lot I have picked there many times. You have to get a hurdle or a piece of wood or board to pick them the other side of the ditch where the best were. Folk have come from the town to gather them. They needed no bridge for they took off shoes and stockings. I am not writing this to find fault, for if a man has work to do he can employ who he will. He is the one that has to pay. But I should like to see the folk who come into the parish to farm, not to think they are all duds that belong to the parish [even] if they are poor. Many persons living in a parish, or belonging to it in [some] way, are satisfied with living where their ancestors lived. It ought not to be that a man buy a parish [and then] he send them all out whether they like it or not.[ii]

Buck Hedging

One winter I and another did a lot of hedging. We must have done a mile or two of what is called buck hedging. This is cut both sides leaving the hedge on top of the bank about half-a-yard or two feet high. We did a long whitethorn hedge of fairly big stuff - straight the fence was. We each cut the top. After it was done it was as straight as could be. The facing cuts all looked as if cut in one, but were not, for many [pieces] were too big. But not many were split either - if one did we used to chaff each another.

---

[i]   Most likely Woody Nightshade - Solanum dulcamarsa.
[ii] A difficult passage – probably means, "*it is not right that a foreman – new to the area – should bypass the local workforce and employ labour from outside the parish.*"

The pattern of differing ages of hedges was not lost on Tulip. Aware that some hedges were ancient he remarks that . . . on many farms the hedges have been done away with [and] new hedges made where they are straight and of thorn and who knows that [*sic* - whether] they are better than at first [i.e. the former] in the long run. For our forebears ordered many hedges and ditches to be put to get the water off so as to drain the land. Plenty were drained by putting wood, straw, picked stones and other material [in them]. But many ditches have been filled up or let go without cleaning them out. The land in places is waterlogged [and] the old drains cannot do their work for they are not clear at the outfall.

Hedge Planting

The fence at that part of Lamsey near to the Old Lamsey Field is a long quickset near on sixty rod or more. This was done by father and son called Chinnery. These were planted late in the season - March before all quicksets were put in - so that many did not grow. [Later] there were privet planted where [the] quickset died. Now, on that long fence where it is the most sandy one can get any amount of rooted privet-set - well rooted if one need to make a hedge or fill up a gap in a hedge. For the small-leaf privet[i] will grow well with cut thorn hedges, for it will trail along both ways. In the garden between my neighbour's and mine, near the house, was a small privet shrub. I laid one or two pieces down, pegged them and put some earth on for the two seasons I was there. The next man who took the house had a privet hedge more than halfway to the road.

Privet hedging

Coppicing and Woodland Work

I worked several winters in a wood. This is nice work when the weather is nice and there is not much snow to tread about in. for when snow is about, wood is mostly bad handling. Me and another man helped to fell the wood. There are several sorts of wood that grow in it - hazel, birch, lime-wood, maple, elm, and others. Principally it was elm. The thatching stuff we used to tie up in full-length bundles - [we also cut] pick stakes,[ii] pea sticks and poles that are fit for making wood hurdles. There are a few more kinds in the wood fit for hurdles, but of no quantity. It is a very bad wood to go about with horses and a wagon for there are lots of pits where pot earth[iii] was formerly dug and carted away. So in a part of the wood [of] about a three acres more or less, there are many holes because the man who had leave to have the earth was not to disturb the trees. But there are not so many trees now [1927] for they were felled during the war for timber. A great many were hauled by traction engines so that a great many hazel stubs were uprooted. It will be some years before the gaps they made will fill up with wood without being planted.

Most likely Wiggery Wood

Brambles and thistles after felling

If one goes into a wood at a time when the under [i.e. undergrowth] has runned [*sic*] up high they will find very little grass or brambles. They can get about fairly well. So they can if it is felled, for the first year, but after they will find in the second year such a jungle as they would not expect. If it was say autumn - early

---

[i] Wild privet, Ligustrum vulgare.
[ii] Perhaps stakes for picket fencing or posts for tethering animals.
[iii] Most likely clay – TR.

41

Blackberries

part - there would be grass [and] boar thistles growing up higher than one could reach and brambles galore. The next year it is dreadful to go through in some parts when there is shooting going on. One has to knock them down and put your foot on them. Some parts you have to go round and what a lot of blackberries I have seen growing on these bushes - beauties. Bushels was once picked one year in this same wood and there are two kinds, one [ripening] a week or two before the other. Then these brambles have done their bit, for if there is a fair amount of underwood they get the master and the brambles die. The vines soon rot and it is clear again for a year or two till it is cut. Where wood is left too long before being felled a good many shrubs die - the best wood grows the most and kills the lesser.

Oak bark for tanning

Bark peeling

I have seen years ago when I have been through a wood, a lot of single young oaks that grew from an acorn. But there seems to be very few in [the one] that we felled and we spoke about it. We had to leave what oak we could and several of those came from a stump that was the foot of a tree. They used to fell a few oaks and peel them for the bark to go to the Halstead tan-yard. Oak is used for tanning leather. When the Byfords first came to the farm [Goldingham Hall] they had a large number of trees put down. There was a timber sale and a number of people to buy. My father helped to peel off the bark etc. At one time if a tree or two had to be felled the men on the farm did them. But since the war started they have men come to do the work. For what reason I cannot say unless they like to pay a lot more money for the job, for there were men on the estate that is in the parish, could fell trees as well as those that come to do the same work. So there was on another large farm or two. I am told this [is] on account of insurance. Woodmen are not under the same class of insurance as are farm workers. Woodmen have more dangerous work. Whether this is the case I do not know, but when tree felling, men needs to be careful - [even] then accidents sometimes occur.

Gang of tree-fellers

Drying bark

At one time the biggest acreage of wood in the parish belonged to the Earl Howe who had an agent to see to the felling of the woods. When the bark-peeling season came along a gang under a foreman was got from the different farms belonging to the estate. But this was not anything to do with the Auberies Estate, who had their own men. The gang between them had all the necessary tools - felling saws, bark spuds - long and short - felling and bough axes. They used to be at work by five in the morning till seven or eight at night [in order] to get the trees peeled before they got bark-bound. I went one or two years, but it was only to do a few trees and only four of us. I enjoyed it, but it is a long day and makes one look for home at night. Bark now is paid for per ton - at one time by the fathom. Then [when peeled] it was set up to bars held up by chourch [*sic* - crotch] sticks. Now it is laid on brush or faggots – the trunk bark on top to keep the wet out. Tops of trees used to be tied up in tits[i] for the making of a special kind of malt. Tied so a faggot could be put in the kiln fire in one [i.e. whole faggot]. But they do not use wood now for they use a smokeless coal - I think the name is anthracite. At one time the agent's man, who was a farmer latterly, let different people buy an acre or more in these woods. Two of my uncles bought a piece at different times. One of them told me that anyone who wanted to [could] get enough thatching stuff to pay for the buying of it. Then it would pay but now [1927] there is not much thatching stuff used. At that time there were more thatching done, but now the use of self-binders make stacks in less numbers [because] they tie corn up tighter.[ii]

---

[i] Tit-faggots – see note page 37.
[ii] See Tulip's comments on self-binder produced sheaves on page 56.

Pruning

Many timber trees are spoiled for not looking after them when young. For a piece cut off a young tree if it is healthy will soon grow over - there is no knot to harm then when the tree is big enough for timber. Willows and poplars should be looked to every year for the first few years. They ought to be done [i.e. pruned, trimmed etc] when the shoots are young. Then they can be done with a knife - one should be carried when the work is being done. Another thing that is needed is a ladder or steps that will not fall over if it does not touch the tree, [for many trees] are not big enough to bare the weight of the ladder. Two men are wanted for the work - one to hold the ladder, for if the ground is uneven it is not safe without being held by someone. Trees done at the right time is time well spent.

Miscellaneous Woodland Crafts.

I often used to turn up a walking stick - one that I had cut out of a hedge. I have done some good sticks. Nice straight ones [in] such as hazel and blackthorn - which can be found at times with good knobs on if one keeps their eyes open. When off a fence and knotted well it makes famous sticks. But the best, or one of the best, was of cherry wood. It grew out of a live piece that was left when the hedge was cut a few years before. The master I then worked for was good to let me have straw that had not been threshed to make beehives with for they look best made with whole straw. So when the threshing machine was at work I cut the wheat-ears off the straw, as I had time or at a mealtime. I gave this stick to him after I had trimmed a good knob, he was pleased with it. He sent it to London [to have] a polish put on and a silver band round it. He then showed it to me - it was a beauty. I have got many sticks in my time and it was no trouble to get rid of them for a trifle, as well as give them away you may be sure.

Walking sticks

Sometimes when we are hedging we find some good rose stems - useful to bud roses on. I have had some good roses, a Marshall Neil, La France and Home Tea roses or Glory John. It was during the early part of my married life, but of late years I have done but very few. Of course at that time there were not such roses as there are at the present day, but they seemed to me to have better middles than now. I saw the loveliest colours of roses this year [1927] I have ever seen before. They have not a good centre when in full bloom, but are lovely in the bud.

Briars for rose budding

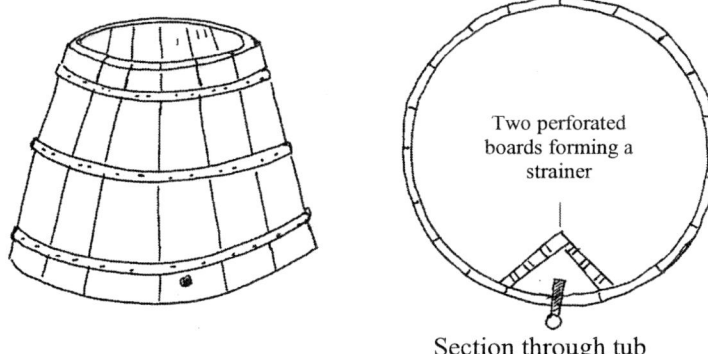

Two perforated boards forming a strainer

Section through tub

Fig 5: A Wort or Mash Tub - from sketches supplied by Tom Rowe.

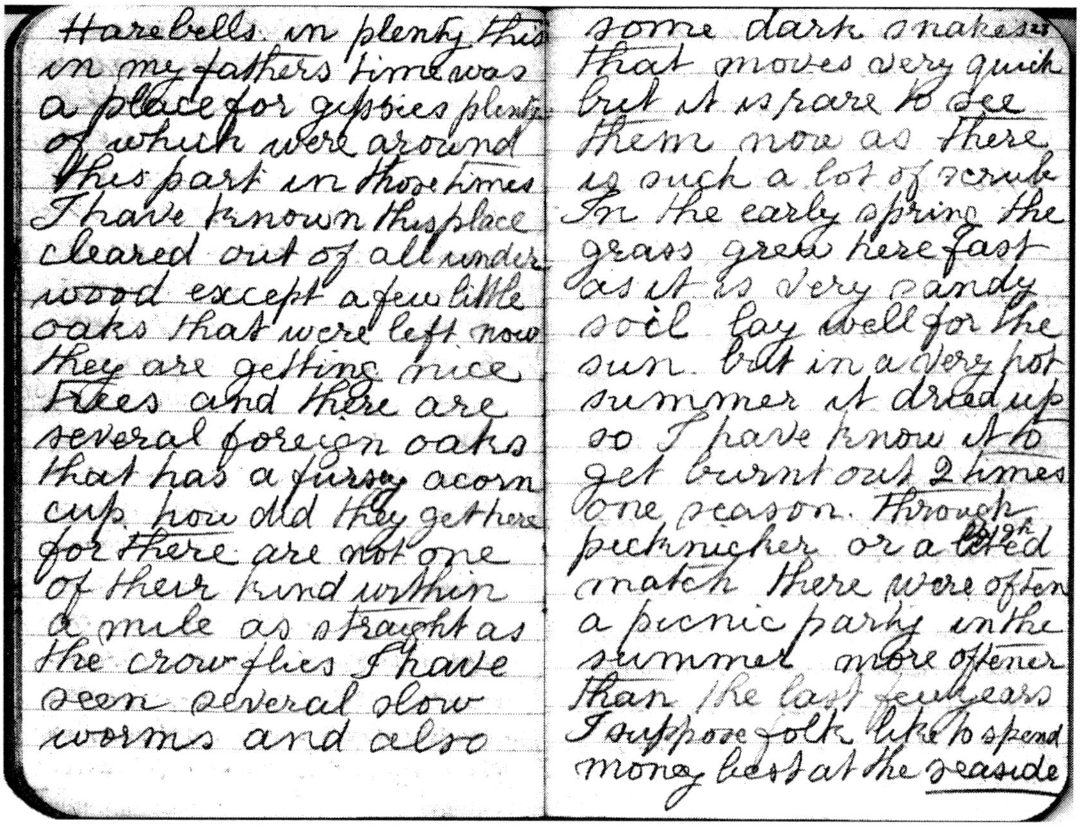

Harebells in plenty this in my fathers time was a place for gypsies plenty of which were around this part in those times I have known this place cleared out of all under wood except a few little oaks that were left now they are getting nice Trees and there are several foreign oaks that has a furry acorn cup how did they get here for there are not one of their kind within a mile as straight as the crow flies I have seen several slow worms and also

some dark snakes that moves very quick but it is spare to see them now as there is such a lot of scrub In the early spring the grass grew here fast as it is very sandy soil lay well for the sun but in a very hot summer it dried up so I have know it to get burnt out 2 times one season. Through picknicher or a lited match there were often a picnic party in the summer more oftener than the last few years I suppose folk like to spend money best at the seaside

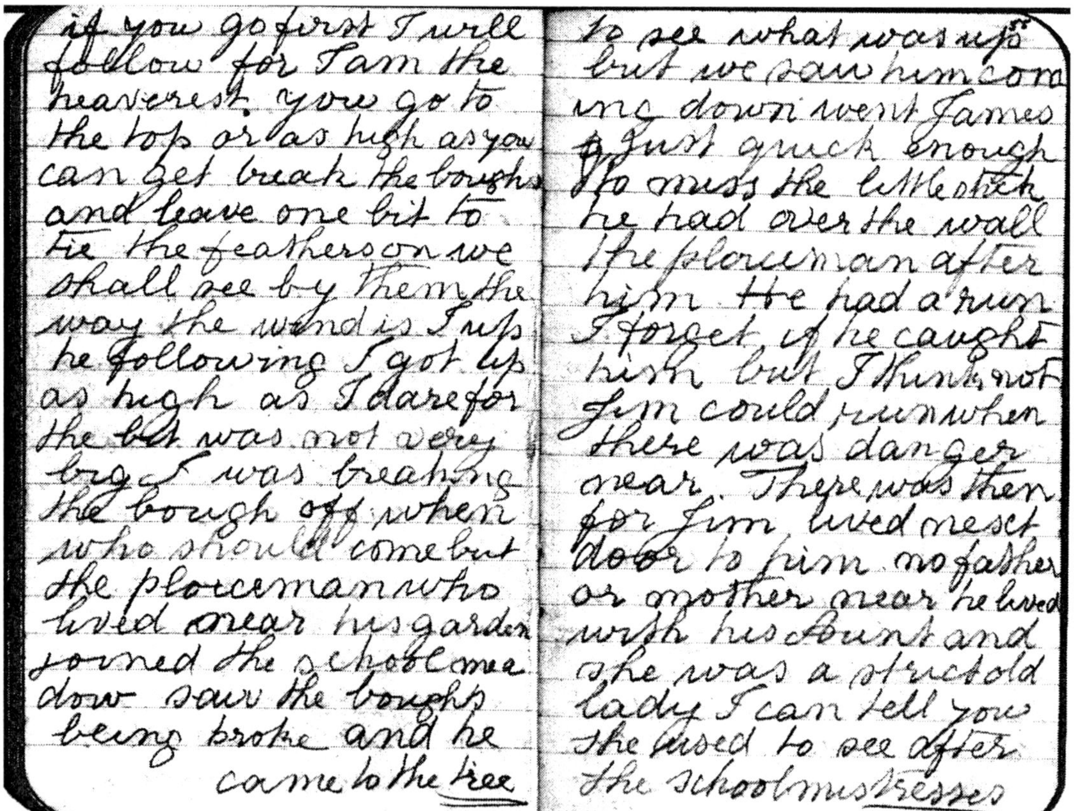

if you go first I will follow for I am the heaverest you go to the top or as high as you can get break the boughs and leave one bit to tie the feathers on we shall see by them the way the wind is I up he following I got up as high as I dare for the but was not very big I was breaking the bough off when who should come but the plowceman who lived near his garden joined the schoolmea dow saw the boughs being broke and he came to the tree

to see what was up but we saw him coming down went James just quick enough to miss the little stich he had over the wall the plowceman after him he had a run I forget if he caught him but I think not Jim could run when there was danger near. There was then for Jim lived next door to him no father or mother near he lived with his Aunt and she was a strict old lady I can tell you she used to see after the schoolmistresses

Fig 6: Facsimile pages from Book III

44

6. ASPECTS OF THE FARMING YEAR

Sowing By hand

No farming is done better nowadays than when first I did harvesting [c1885] and till there was so much machinery to do without manual labour. Think of the difference in farming in a man's time if he be eighty years of age. At one time, say one hundred years ago or very little more, farmers used to have the corn sown by hand, either dibbed or sown broadcast. If dibbed, a man would work two rows, he going backwards so as not to fill in the holes he had made. There were two droppers, for they were very good that could drop corn for two dibbers.

Dibbed corn

Wheat on allotments was dibbed or broadcasted. This broadcast seed is thrown about over the top and then has to be forked in – not deep of course. I see some done one day this season [1937]. I said to the man who I knew well – he is seventy – "So you are doing a bit of old England's job in sowing so."
"Yes," he said.
"How much do you sow now as it is so late?"
"Two bushel".[i]
"I should have thought half a bushel more for birds etc."
"There will be enough," he said. Yes, good land and it do fairly well if it is covered well. He said that it covered well by being harrowed to finish. I asked if they were going to cross-harrow it. "No."

Broadcast corn

On my father's patch where one third was sown with wheat he used to dib it. He was fairly good. He have seen plenty done, for he had dropped wheat behind dibbers. The men who were good dibbers used to do about half an acre per day. They dibbed along the stetches,[ii] so many rows on a four-yard stetch. Perhaps they started in the middle. Then the furrows were not sown. I believe some rows were ten inches apart. These men had two droppers. I have been told times of a woman, who is now some bit over eighty, who could drop behind her father, Sam Butcher, and keep up. Why it was dibbed was so that it could be close-hoed, for if broadcast it could only be chopped over.

Wheat on father's allotment

The Tools of the trade

Nearly all corn was hoed and picked over with a hoe, spud or weeding hook. I did some one year when I was between fifteen and sixteen years of age, with another mate a year older than me. We did a great many acres at 1/- per acre. When the corn was wet so we could not work in it, we singled mangolds and turnips at the same rate of pay and we did well. No one to look after us. Had we been on day work he would have had 7/- per week and I should have had 6/-. We mostly worked it so we had 2/- per week more, with a shower given in[iii] - no one to say ought to us. On that farm if one used a hoe, 2d was allowed for hoe money to have it sharpened or re-laid. At that time a wheat hoe was sharpened for 1 ½d and a bean hoe for 2d. And it paid to have them done for ease, for it make a deal of difference to both man and master. Although at the same time I have known some young married men [who] when told by their mates that it was a poor hoe, would

Weeding corn

Sharpening hoes

---

[i] Arthur Young's book on Suffolk Agriculture states two bushels per acre as the usual rate, or sometimes a peck more than this – AC.
[ii] A stetch was the ploughed land between two furrows.
[iii] Probably a reference to loss of wages in wet weather. See note page 49.

say. "It's good enough for me, I am not going to spend money to have it sharpened." He would had I been the master - I should look to that. Such as him are no workmen and never will be good ones, for the best workmen have the best tools.

Hand hoeing wheat

In the spring – it used to be more in the early part – nearly all farmers had a lot of wheat hoed. A good thing too for wheat to be thin, and if moulded up it branches out better and also it kill a lot more weeds. On some land if it is sown early and the ground is in good tilth, there is a lot of winter weed and a sort of mardlings[i] that grows. If left the wheat goes yellow. It is only a surface weed but it do a lot of harm. It used to be said, 'an acre of wheat hoed, [produced] a comb more'. If so it certainly paid to do for that crop, as hoeing was let at 4/6 per acre. I know if a thistle is cut as soon as out of the ground, it will not grow above the corn to bloom and blow about when ripe. A man can cut thistles much faster with a hoe than with a weeding hook that cuts about one or two at a time. Not only does it do good to the crop, but with a hoe one can cut several with a stroke. Look at such seedlings as docks and thistles, for they are seedlings [at] sometime, although a thistle will spread under ground by a long tuber and this will often lay just below where the plow cuts. It used to be gone over by boys or an old man with a pail to take the dock roots out. The best way, for a dock will grow by only lying on top of the land. Those ones seed the earliest, for ones that are deep are turned right over with the furrow and they do not get out so quick. One year my brother and I was set to cut the docks in wheat below the crowns. We had our hoes set to diggen,[ii] so as to chop deep after them. There was a lot of them and we were told to do it well. We did and there were very few that ripened in the wheat when cut. Of course the roots were there, but it stopped the seeding of them. That way we could do a great many more than could be taken up, for digging up docks is a slow job. It did not matter much about the roots as the next year the land was fallowed.

Cutting thistles

Cutting docks

Mangold and turnip hoeing

Soon after there is mangold and turnip hoeing, where one needs a wider hoe. These all cost money for men find them mostly [i.e. use their own]. But something ought to be allowed to sharpen and relay them. If I were a farmer I would see to that. A man should have good hoes, [because] not only does a man get over more ground much easier, but to have to cut twice at a weed is something to think of.

Farm workers' tools

There is so many kinds of work on a farm, so a day labourer wants a lot of tools. I will tell of these as well as I can. Horsemen do not want quite so many, as the tools that are wanted for the most part come with such machines as plows, drills, wagons, carts, corn reapers and grass cutting machines. But when there is little horse work to do they have to do other work. He, like his fellow day-man wants tools. I will take from harvest till it is upon us again.

After harvest there are fields to clear round. A man will want a rip[iii] and a scythe - an old one, a bush scythe, is best for it is short. A master I worked for bought two – good things they were. As well as cutting grass such a tool will cut a piece of wood as big as your finger and not come to harm. A fork is also needed to pick it

Rips and scythes

---

[i] Mardlings – *Chenopodium album* – also called Muckweed.
[ii] A set hoe was probably one made by the blacksmith to a specification, TR, who also remembered using an old cut-throat razor tied to the end of a handle to cut thistles.
[iii] A large sickle-type tool without the teeth. Also known as a bagging hook.

up out of the way for burning. A rip is 2/- or 2/6 and mind you do not break it. I do not know the cost of a bush scythe.

There is manure to get on the land. A manure fork is best for filling and spreading.

After the fields are sown there are furrows and outlets to clean out and corners used to be digged up and sown. A shovel and fork is needed to clean out a water furrow. A fork, a digging one, is used to dig the corners out, as a manure fork is not fit for digging if too wet and sloshy. Of course a two-pronged fork is used when there is machining [threshing] to do.

When the leaves are off, there are the hedges to cut off and tie up. We used to tie up all the bushes for oven stuff to bake bread with, but scarcely anyone bake now.[i]

Hedging

Before the turnips are finished being hoed comes hay time and trefoil or trefolium seedtime. Then white clover seed comes before harvest. Of course most of this is cut by a grass mowing machine, but we used to mow it [by hand] and I should think that is best, for a man mows a swarth of two yards in width. If mown it can be cut for the most part when a bit damp. Machines do not work as well as when dry. Also the horses trample on a lot and if ripe it shell out. There is less turning on mowed hay and it is easier to gather in most cases. All such seed needs careful handling as they all shell so easy. If hot and dry much seed is lost. To mow such stuff a man wants a good scythe. A new one if a good one needs less sharpening. A scythe is an expensive tool now. I have bought a new kiltre[ii] for 5/6. Though now I am told a new one is £1. There are several items to a scythe. First the blade or grass hook, the ferrule, the heel wedge, the scythe stick and the two throwls [i.e. handles] - without the bail. If one cuts wheat with it he has a wheat bail or rake to keep the corn straight - and straight it can be laid with it,[iii] but one cannot use it in standing corn or near a hedge when cutting round. Of course during the harvest time men do need very many tools extra. If one look in a catalogue to see the prices of such tools as I have mentioned they will find that several shillings will be wanted to pay for them and the more they are used the more they wear out and then a new one is wanted. I did not mention the utensils that are needed to sharpen them with, but there are a lot more now than before the war [1914-18].

Hay time

Scythes

Of threshing and barn work

I will mention another tool that is used very little and that is a flail [frail] - a tool to thresh with. There are several pieces wanted to fit one up. There is the handstaff and the swongel[iv] or the thick piece of wood that is swung on to the corn and the box cap or swivel. A thick piece of leather is laced on the swingel and this thong joins the swingel to the box cap and hand-staff.[v] An old man used to make a box cap with a piece of ash for about 1/-. Several men used to make them for themselves. I have made a few, one for a flail and two or three for a

Flails

---

i   For Tulip's comments on hedging tools see chapter 5.
ii   The complete scythe TR. The component parts of any tool or implement EDD.
iii See Fig 7, page 68.
iv Also known as a swingle or swipple.
v   Several methods for fixing these were employed. Tulip's was probably similar to Fig 8, page 68, an Essex example.

Flailing beans

Flailing beans for seed

Barn work

band-maker.[i] Men used to thresh out all corn with a flail. If it were done now I should not think it would cost near so much again as it does to do it by machine. But this is not worth the thinking about. But were I a farmer who growed beans or a special kind of peas I should have them threshed by flail, for very dry beans if threshed by machine will break. Broken beans will not grow. If the beans are not hard as is sometimes the case in a showery harvest, they will be bruised and they will not grow. So this is the best way if a farmer wants beans to sow. A few loads or more should be carted as dry as possible and placed where they are handy or put in a barn. These beans will thresh well with a flail and not be bruised or split. They will grow. Beans that are podded fairly well thresh well. A man would do nearly two sacks a day. But anyway it would not be all loss of time for there are days that men could not work abroad. That would be a time to have that done. I knew a place where all beans were threshed that way so the men had always something to do when the weather was not fit for outside work. I have heard say that the barn men who was threshing from one harvest to another was angry if they were taken out of the barn. [They earned] 1/- per comb for wheat and 10d for barley ready for market. Not much money, but that was not in my time. This reminds me of my grandfather. I have heard my uncle say more than once that his father was so [disposed that] he could not do horseman work. So he was a barn man and my uncle as a boy worked with him [c1830s] with a little flail and did other jobs at times - to sift the corn or turn the sheaves in the bay of the barn and help him generally.

Cleaning and separating the grain

It seems a marvel to folk now how corn used to be fanned clean enough for market. But all used to be done that way. The fan is a wicker made scoop, made very strong and wove very closely so that a wheat kernel could not stay in the fan. Scarcely dust would go through it is so fine. Clover seed, especially the white, is very small. To get it clean it used to be throwed on a cloth with a wood[en] corn shovel. Only a good barn man could do it, such a delicate job it was. A neighbouring farmer would borrow a good man if he had no one on his own farm that could throw seed - so I have heard. These shovels were made of poplar wood all in one piece. But the totles [i.e. handles] for one-hand mud scoops are made of the same kind of wood. Mud do not stick to wood as it do to iron or metal.

Samples

Measuring corn

Wheat was dressed before it was sown. Of this I will write. From the dressing machine it went perhaps to a blower, then a sample had to be taken from the heap of corn to be marketed. Yes a sample should be taken from parts of the said heap of corn or the bulk may not be the same as the sample. After being sold corn was then put up by the bushel, four bushels to the sack, struck level. Potatoes, turnips, apples, pears etc three bushels to the sack, if used. Now it is done by weight. The best and fairest for all. For when corn was put up by the bushel it was done lightly in my part. Not as in Holy Writ - pressed, shaken and heaped. No. So if a man on a farm was light handed in the putting up of corn he was valued by so doing. How about the buyer? For I myself have put up corn both ways with fault or none. As always the buyer wants as much as he can get for money and the seller as little for most money - the [same the] whole world over. Nothing wrong in it perhaps, but why blame those who has the doing of the work if told to do so. Yes a lot of humbug to put the blame on those who do the job. It makes me think of a man putting up wheat in a barn. The master comes into the barn, says to the man,

---

[i] PR suggests that this might well be the maker or user of the brace-type tool used for winding straw rope – see *Made in England*, Dorothy Hartley, 1939. The EDD says that a band-maker is one who makes straw bands with which to tie sheaves at harvest time.

"John this wheat has made a good price. I do not want you to put a kernel too much in." "No Sir." John said. "I had to halve one just now to make it come right." "Well," he said, "I do not want you to be quite so near as that." So you quite see Reader why I say weighing in the best. For I know one man I worked for was the nearest man for weight as ever I had to do with. When once I asked him the reason. "Why Philip," he answered, "they never give me anything that I do not know, especially if I put it on this machine." And that was good one. It was kept in good order and he saw to it that it was so kept, for that machine could weigh in ounces.

Weighing corn

Deep snow, rats and threshing

When talking of the deep snow of Thursday 27th November 1889, mentioned above, Tulip says . . . I was working at Armsey Farm. Well a bean stack were to be threshed - not a big stack. This day the machine was set to thresh winter beans. We were allowed 6d per day when working with machine and some other work. Only the roof of the stack was threshed that day as it snowed so heavily. A lot of us men had a fire in an old bake-house belonging to the farm. A man who was the stockman lived in the house with an invalid wife. The daughter was a dressmaker who played the organ or music at Great Henny church. We men - if I could be called as such for I was only eighteen and did not think myself one, although many times I had to take the place of one - kept there all day. It was a rule, for if one was on the farm when the weather was so we could not work and anything important was to do, the foreman could see that it was done. Our wages were not stopped if on the place.[i] Next morning we young men went to see if the lot of rats we expected there to be in the stack had made any tracks in the snow. Not a sign of a rat could any of us four or five see. Between ourselves we said that perhaps a stoat or weasels had drove the rats away before the machine were set.

Armsey Farm

Threshing

The snow was raked off the roads and around the machine sometime in the morning. Sometime before dinner the stack, not being very big, was nearly finished. Presently there was a "view halloo" from the men who were on the stack putting the bean sheaves onto the machine. It was one sheaf off the bottom [or bed of] straw that was laid down to keep the bean sheaves from getting damp or wet. We had stopped up all the rat holes around the bottom before we began to thresh. The sport had begun. Plenty of rats. All told when finished there were seventy-two rats large and small that could run about. That was all right between us. Seventy-two pennyworth of beer beside what we were allowed for the work. "Philip." The engine driver said to me, "You can go and get the beer. You know where?" So off I go. From where we were it was roughly half a mile. There had been very little traffic on either road or path, for the corset makers who went from the village did not turn out - only those that were obliged to. Thus it was rather bad walking for me, but downhill. I soon got there [The King's Head, Ballingdon] and asked for 6/- worth of beer at 1/- per gallon. So they put up the beer in a cask. A nine gallon one I believe, for a pin or half size would not hold six gallons. They always gave some beer to those who fetched a good lot. I drank the beer they gave me against a good fire.

Rat money for beer

Getting the beer

When ready I made a start up the Ballingdon Hill. I put the cask between my two shoulders and started up this long hill. It is I should say some bit more than half a

Carrying beer up Ballingdon Hill

---

[i] Many men lost wages when unable to work in wet weather.

mile. A nice long hill folk say. I was not cold I can tell you when I got to the farm with those six gallons of beer. Of course I had a bit of help when I got to a gate, for I rested the load on the top of the gate till I was ready for another move. I think I rested twice. I got to the machine not much later than I could help for I knew the men were waiting for the rat beer. I think I left it in the engine house[i] as that was usually our bar. When I told the engine driver that the beer was back he called to the others and said, "Beer mates." For the rat money usually went to his account when threshing. When rats were caught by others at various jobs it was up to them to take the money, for all rats were paid for ld per rat. When the men got to the bar or engine house the driver said, "Did you bring the lot Philip?" "Yes." "Why I did not think you would for so many, for half would have been enough for this time." I said, "I thought I was to bring as much as the rats come to." "Well it will be drunk I dare say." It was too - that day. How stiff and sore I was the next morning with that load and walk I can tell you.[ii] I did not feel like running as I had to do, if behind.

A note on Elevens or Beavers [iii]

There are some farms where they do not stop the threshing machines for elevens or beavers as it is called. But I think if masters were to be on a corn or straw stack or doing any other kind of work with a machine, especially if they thresh a hundred comb a day, they would want a bite to eat and a pint of good beer if they got to work at 7 o'clock and kept on till midday. If I had my way they should try it and see. I know some of them would say they could do it. So they could I know. So they ought to for they live much better than men who have a wife and three or four children to keep. They would find the tail was on the other pig if they were served the same way.

Working in severe conditions

The snow I mentioned came too early for farmers who kept a lot of stock. The mangolds were got off and clamped, even if not all earthed up as they nearly all did at that time - the best too if there be sharp frosts and usually it always freezes if snow is about, especially if the weather is clear. At Armsey farm, where I was working, the swedes were not pulled, let alone carted. This and the home farm, [The Auberies] was worked as one, excepting there were horsemen at both places. They kept three horsemen, two of whom were at the home farm.

Armsey Farm

I was told off [*sic*][iv] with an old man called Matthew Halls. I liked working with him for he could tell some tales of the Auberies and Armsey as well as his native village, Belchamp Walter. His tales of Belchamp and of the old Squire Raymond went back many years. The bailiff or foreman told me that what he wanted me to do was, "Not a nice job Philip, but it has to be done so we will make the best of it." When I went to the field I found that the old chap had already done some of the swede turnings. Although the snow had settled down a bit we could not see the tops of the turnips, but where the rows were the snow was higher because it laid on the turnips. I think he had a hoe to pull or chop the tops off and then

Squire Raymond

---

[i] This may have been a horse engine house – the text is not clear.

[ii] the weight of six gallons @ 9lbs per gallon. Therefore Tulip carried a half-hundredweight on his back! AC.

[iii] Elsewhere the following note appears, 'we had breakfast before we went to work. We used to have elevenses or as some folk call it in Suffolk, 'Beaver'.

[iv] Dialect term meaning to be asked or instructed to work with someone.

chopped them up, but I cannot say now for we used two or three different kinds of tool to find out which was the best both to get over the job and for our ease. For one can make their own work harder by not using the tools fit or best to do the said job, be it what it may. I know I soon went to the blacksmith to get him to make me a tool so I could do the work with gloves on. To get gloves wet soon spoil them. They also are cold too if wet. I believe we were on that job till near Christmas, unless we had to go for threshing or any other kind of work. If it had rained we could shelter or go to the farm. There was snow about a long time that year, also the early part of the next year.

Digging up or, what is more likely, gathering the tops of swedes

Of Horses

My father was a horseman at a large farm [Goldingham Hall] where there were a place where the men who worked near had their meals. This place was called the collar hole. This had a wide seat two parts on two sides and in the place under, old used plough shares were put. There were tags for harness, principally horse collars and the other gear. There were the initials in chalk where the men sat, so every man kept to his place. A granary being over the top with a stepladder. The funny part is that if the wind came from full west it was opposite the collar hole door. The wind did not go in unless a stable door was open, then it was windy inside.

The Goldingham Hall collar hole

On Jenkins farm three good horseboxes were made to keep entire horses.[i] My uncle [Charles] had the privilege of having them made to his order. He had them built a rod square inside. Fine horseboxes they are - if still used as such - with two hefty half doors. Once when he had two stallions, one in the yard outside in the night, one in the stable, those two got together by one kicking the doors. The thick bolt shot back on the under door so that both horses got together. I suppose they fought but was not heard nearby. Although a half a mile or more westward a man heard and asked what was amiss. These two horses were screaming a lot. When my uncle went to them in the morning those two horses were in a plight, bit and kicked about ever so. The skin broken at places with hair off. He did not wish his master to see them. It was hot weather so he dressed the places as well as he could. When he got to the field he cut boughs etc so he neatly covered up the horses with them, knowing if he could get by the day with the two horses he could do to them for the morrow, so the places would not look so conspicuous. His master came, but the horses you are sure were restless as there were plenty of flies and my uncle had no wish for a talk with his master today. He liked him best at a distance.

Stallions fighting at Jenkins Farm

I know once my uncle told me when Mr. Badham came from Suffolk he wanted to make his men do as they do in Suffolk. In Suffolk they used to turn out horses first thing in the morning and keep in the fields all day with the horses till the day's work with the horses was done. The men had a bit of food and drink if they took it. The horses were not taken off the plow or other implement they were on. This is what Mr. Badham wished the Bulmer men to do. Now my uncle was as me. Let them do what they will in Suffolk, but the Essex men say they do their work as well as the others so why alter things. So to make my uncle see his way was the best he said, "Charles. Look at the hunters, they go off in the morning and don't have any food till they get home - sometimes that is late." 'Hm,' said my

The horseman's day – Suffolk versus Essex system

---

[i] Entire horses – breeding stallions.

51

uncle. "Don't tell me anything about fox hunters. They just ride from one public house to another." "Yes Charles, but if they do they are not gentlemen." He left my uncle at that.

Mr. Badham

This Mr. Badham was a very good farmer. He bought a good many straw stacks around, for he undertook to find straw for manure for Allen Bros of Ballingdon, who kept upward of a hundred horses for their business of coal, chalk, sand, malt and bricks. They had a great business in those days before the railway came to Sudbury. Also it was a few years after that, the railway was across the commons to Long Melford. So there was a great business for horses of conveying around Sudbury. Beside there being some other very long journeys at this time or about for my father remembers the railway coming to Sudbury from Marks Tey.

Jenkins Farm

This manure that was taken from all these horses was put on a heap or in a large bin. This used to heat the straw but not get it rotten. That would be taken to the farm, put into the yards and very soon was taken out again. So land was good. Also he had little land but what was cropped, for there were at that time a little over two hundred acres with some meadows. There were near three hundred at the time I worked on the same farm, but Tye Corner Farm and 'The Plough' land was by then included in the whole.

Mr. Badham the innovative farmer

This Mr. Badham was a pioneer of machinery on the farms around. He had the first steam threshing tackle - also a machine for grass and clover cutting as well as the first for cutting wheat. That farm kept up the distinction of having the first agricultural tools till long after I worked there first for Mr. D. Gardiner.

Mr. Badham was also an exhibitor of horses and stock. Also he gave prizes through the societies for stacking, furrow drawing and stetch plowing. He also was very particular of hedges and gates being left open or anything untidy about the farm. He used to tell the plowmen to take up [i.e. remove] crouch or twitch grass when they were at plough - but they did not stop a plough for that very often.

Agricultural shows, horse shows and Suffolk Punches

Suffolk horses

My uncle [Charles] had the management of his Suffolk stallions. Sometimes there were four there and a young one or two. Both my uncle and my father had a lot to do with agricultural shows. My uncle took a horse to the first Royal Agricultural Show, which was held at Windsor. I feel sure it was in the year 1900 [that] he went to a Jubilee Show of the same also at Windsor. He got on for a scavenger[i] time the show was on. It was there that a gentleman, Mr. W. Byford, had a very good Suffolk horse that took a special prize as well as first prize I feel sure. Mr Byford sold this horse time the show was on for a good sum of money. But the horse died at Windsor. My uncle said this was the first show many Suffolk horses had silver manes. Now one sees but very few silver manes on Suffolk horses. Also I do not think that studbooks were out as now. My uncle told me that horses were tied to stakes, no canvas above as now. My father has told me he went to a show at Fakenham in Norfolk. He had to stay by his horse all day unless relieved by someone he knew. So if it rained as it did sometimes it was a poor job.

---

[i] Most likely employed to clear litter etc.

Also my uncle said that once at a show his horse brought home £75 in prizes. That horse won the special prize £25, The Town Prize and The County Prize, £20 each, [or] £40. £5 if the horse had travelled in the County and £5 for the breeder of the horse. Mr. Badham bred him. Thus £75 that horse won or had the money paid for him. I think the horse's name was Emperor.

Also another tale worth repeating perhaps. A horse under uncle's care had the misfortune of loosing his mane. He was booked to exhibit at a show. I cannot say where now. That horse went to the show and won first prize. In the newspaper of show events it was said that Mr. Badham's horse won first prize not withstanding a flowing false mane. When brood mares came to the farm for stud my uncle had a lad who attended. If the right coloured horses came my uncle would say. "Boy they are the sort." Then my uncle would go round to The Plough [Inn] with the groom that came with the horses. Both would have some beer and perhaps food if a meal time. This boy would get the hair from out the mane or tail for a purpose my uncle wanted it for.[i] There were many horses that came often on Sundays if man and master liked. One can be sure of that for neither men nor horses worked a lot on Sunday, but that which was necessary and going to stud with horse was. Also pubs kept open all day at that time for travellers. So beer helped some along to the farm.

Horse with false mane

Removing horses hair

I could fill up of tales and experiences of that my uncle has told me, for he has travelled with entire horses through Essex and Suffolk a very great deal. Also he travelled a part of Surrey both sides of The Hog Back, to the farms on either side.

---

[i] Probably collected to add to, or make a false mane for another horse – or some other specialist use for finest horse hair – PR.

Some notes on lineal measure.
To avoid confusion abbreviations, not symbols, for feet and inches are used in the text.
Thus, inch = in., foot = ft., and yard = yd.
1 inch = 25.4 mm; 12 inches = 1 ft = 30.48 cm and 3 feet = 1 yard or .9144 M.
1 rod, pole or perch = 5 ½ yards or 5.0292 M.
A chain = 22 yards or 4 rods, poles or perches.

Some notes on pre-metric currency.
There are some inconsistencies in the originals between Tulip's use of numerals, words and symbols: the following notes explain.
Symbol for (old) penny = d. 12 (old) pennies = 1 shilling or 5 new pence.
Old pence without shillings are written thus: 1d, 6d, etc.
Old shillings and pence are written thus: 1/- = one shilling, 2/6 = two shillings and six pence.

Map 2   BULMER IN TULIP'S TIME
Farms, fields and woods mentioned in text

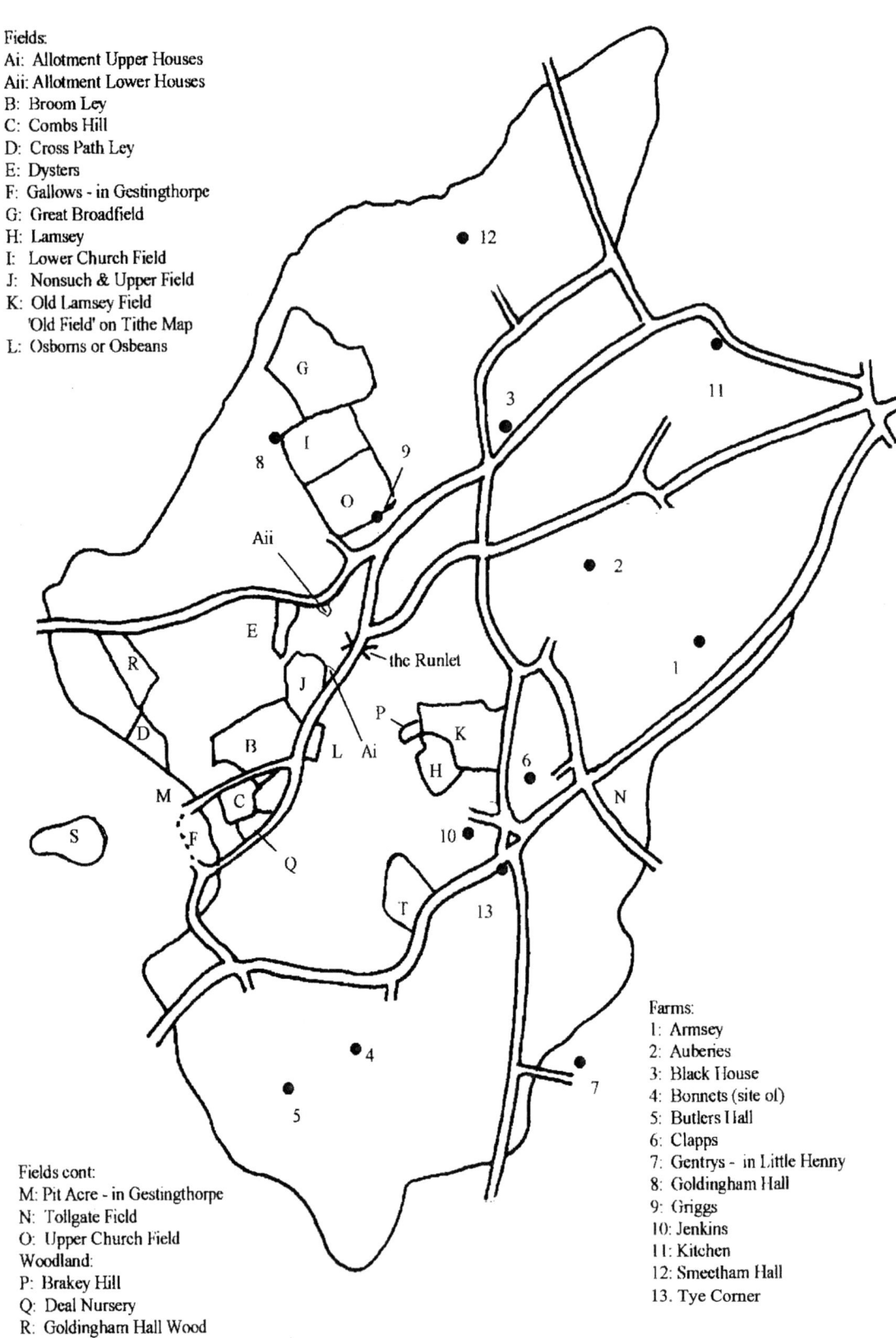

Fields:
Ai: Allotment Upper Houses
Aii: Allotment Lower Houses
B: Broom Ley
C: Combs Hill
D: Cross Path Ley
E: Dysters
F: Gallows - in Gestingthorpe
G: Great Broadfield
H: Lamsey
I: Lower Church Field
J: Nonsuch & Upper Field
K: Old Lamsey Field
   'Old Field' on Tithe Map
L: Osborns or Osbeans

Fields cont:
M: Pit Acre - in Gestingthorpe
N: Tollgate Field
O: Upper Church Field
Woodland:
P: Brakey Hill
Q: Deal Nursery
R: Goldingham Hall Wood
S: Wiggery Wood
T: Parsons Wood

Farms:
1: Armsey
2: Auberies
3: Black House
4: Bonnets (site of)
5: Butlers Hall
6: Clapps
7: Gentrys - in Little Henny
8: Goldingham Hall
9: Griggs
10: Jenkins
11: Kitchen
12: Smeetham Hall
13. Tye Corner

7. HARVESTING

Scythes, sickles and reapers

George Badham farmed Jenkins until his death in November 1877. The following incident probably took place in the 1850s. Whether David and Charles Rowe were directly involved is not clear, but Charles, twenty years older than his brother, was in Badham's employ and reckoned that the following was about the only good idea George Badham brought from Suffolk.

Mr. Badham brought some things from Suffolk which uncle did not find fault with. For wheat was cut by sickle in Bulmer. In Suffolk where Mr. Badham farmed the men there used a scythe to cut wheat with. He had a man come from Suffolk to demonstrate on the scythe and showed how they did it. They started cutting wheat with the scythe and after the men got used to it they liked it, for [with a sickle] it took a man, if a good hand, three days to cut an acre of wheat. With a scythe [fitted with] the wheat rake of the Suffolk type I do not know how much the men did, for of course they all had to get used to the scythe and the heavy rake they had on the scythe at the start. But I have heard both my uncle and my father say that twelve men had been in a twelve acre field and they had cut the field in one day and have set it up in rows, shocked or traved. A good day's work. So one man if he used the scythe all day would have cut two acres if his mate had tied up two.

First use of scythe for cutting wheat in Bulmer

At that time all land laid [was cultivated] on a four yards stetch - no corn [was sown] in [the] furrows. Also in the middle of a stetch they had a wide way and all the corn was cut if possible as the stetches were. So a man with his scythe cleared just the half [of the stetch] if not too much to reach for [and] the man who followed cut that extra ringe[i] of wheat. My father did not say strong wheat but good wheat standing well, [was best to harvest] not [that] laid or beaten by wind and wet. One day Mr. Badham came to the men and told them that a machine was got up to cut the wheat. A man in the company said, "But they will not get one to tie it up Sir, will they?" "Oh yes they will get a machine to do that." Of course the men laughed for they thought that impossible. Who would not?

All barley was cut with a scythe. It did not take long to cut a field. Sixteen men with scythes cut down a field a quarter mile long taking two yards each. Many carried a swarth[ii] of 7ft and some farms had stetches called eights. If these were 8ft, it was wide [for one man] to cut if strong. The scythe I should say was set out wider. I have been told these were cut at one time, one man to one stetch. Of that I have never seen. But two men can easily reach a four-yard stetch. Barley is cut usually the best way according to how it lie or is blown about by the wind. Then if possible it was cut across the stetches.

Barley cut with scythe

Once my father with the harvesters of Goldingham Hall, about sixteen men with two halfmen,[iii] reaped little Gallows Field with sickles. The first and only field I

Field cut with sickles

---

[i] Row or ridge – EDD.

[ii] The row of mown grass or corn which falls from the scythe – EDD.

[iii] Boys and youths were half or three-quarter men under the age of eighteen. See also page 59 below.

ever saw reaped [by hand]. Why did they reap it? Because to get the machine there it was a mile or more from the home farm and not much wheat grew near this field that year. This way it could be carted and finished right away. Also if cut with scythes it would have to be horse raked, which was a long way to go after such a small field of two acres. Most of the men had used sickles before and knew how to use them. They also thought it would be best in the long run as it was a showery time. My father was Lord, or leading man. The next one My Lady.[i]

Sail Reapers

The reaping machine usually had three horses to take it round the field as it cut the corn and one or two of the four sails or arms had a kind of rake on, two were dummy. The two with rakes sweeping the corn off the platform onto the ground out of the way for [*sic* - of] the machine and horses when they came round the field the next time; and so on till the field was finished. This machine did not carry the corn round the corners, so it was kicked about by the horses a lot. That made bad tying at the corners. On some farms a man was told off to be at each corner to tie so machine and horses should not tread the corn to make it bad for tying. But all men are not fair to their master or their mates, for out of sight out of mind they slacked their duty. I say it is up to a man to do right. And surely it is not right for a man to rest if his mates are working hard to get the harvest in when it is fine; for harvesting is not good to do in the rain.

The first Self-binding Machine in Bulmer

Near Upper Houses

Broom Ley was the first field that I saw a self-binder at work. It was in July 1882 when this field of early Talavera wheat was fit to cut. A machine that came to that field was said to come from America.[ii] I was only ten years or a little over at the time. When we got home from school we went to the field to see the machine that cut and tied at the same time. It tied with twine. That machine was brought by a man of Acton I think, named Leech, as he had no corn ripe enough to cut. The machine was sent for and the man came with it so he might demonstrate so as to sell more of these self-binders for farmers to use. It did the work well. The wheat was not strong, but good, standing up well so the machine could cut and tie all round the piece [selected area] of wheat that had [previously] been cut through and around by scythe [for machine access]. There were many people who came to see this machine after their day's work was over.

Making straw 'bands' or 'withes' to tie up sheaves

This early white Talavera wheat used to be bad to tie up behind a sail reaper for the stem is brittle. After it is cut and lay a day or so in the sun and wind, it breaks its band as bad as any wheat I know without [*sic* - except when] the wheat is dead ripe. When I have been tying such wheat I had to make two or three bands before it would hold. Nowadays there is very little tied by hand, but the corn is not in such good condition as then, for a self-binding machine cut and ties as it goes

Carting unripe wheat

along. If there is green stuff [weeds etc.] in [the sheaf], and in some seasons there are plenty, the machine ties it up tight. The green stuff that is in the middle if set up on wet ground do not 'make' as the saying is. Yes, they get to cart it and must do for there is a lot to do. We must not wait or there will be rain and we cannot cart the wheat. But it is not fit to cart unless the farmer do not want to have it

Of binders tying sheaves too tightly

---

[i] For Lord and Lady of the Harvest - see below.
[ii] For a full account of early harvesting machinery see *Our Mother Earth*, Ashley Cooper, 1998.

56

threshed till the summer. And what has happened? The wheat got hot and the green stuff fermented. The wheat had a nasty smell and it is only fit for grinding purposes, for it is musty. Now had that wheat been cut with a sail reaper or scythe and if it had been tied as soon as cut it would not have been tied so tight. The wind and sun could get into the sheaves. They are not so even - they are rougher than sheaves machine tied, for the rollers and packers on the machine do it neater, but not better for the corn. For hand tied sheaves do not pack so tight on the stack and the wind will blow the dry through. Also if it has laid in the field a day or two or more the green has seared up. Such stacks do not get hot.[i] Maybe a bit warm if it is a hot day when they are carted - then the sun is stacked in and it is sure to be warm. Such stacks as are carted and done that way are always fit to thresh in a month or so. The corn will be nosey[ii], but will be as the God Almighty intended it should be for the food of man. Other corn should be treated in the same way. It would pay for the extra shillings it would make per quarter.

Of course there were not many self-binders come into the parish, I should say for nearly ten years after that date. When they were tried they failed, for there is a vast difference in corn growing in England and America. First, wheat in America is not sown till spring, say April, then not fit to cut as early as in England, where the majority of wheat is sown in the autumn. No wheat sown in April can come up to wheat sown in October I know. Why, in England, where land is done well by those good farmers [as] there are in Essex and Suffolk, the part I know so well, they grow more sacks per acre than is done in America in bushels. For there is no country in the World can beat England in the growing of corn. Believe me Readers, I have known of wheat.

Essex faming compared with that in America

My uncle told me when he came home from [a show at] Windsor, how he heard a gentleman from America tell another gentleman of how there was a machine used there that cut, threshed, weighed and dropped the corn in a pair of bags. [It] did that as it went around the field. Seeing my uncle interested he came to him and told him what he had to the other gentleman.

Rumour of the first American combines

Yields

I have heard many times by those who knew, that this Talavera wheat that growed in Broom Ley for Mrs. Byford's executors in 1882, when threshed it came out at ten sacks [22.5 cwt.] per acre - twenty-seven acres to this field. But I have known of ten acres sown with a special wheat on my brother Albert's farm in Bulmer. My brother Sid drilled it with another man. He told me it came to a little over one hundred and sixty sacks or combs [i.e.36 cwt., per acre]. I asked my brother if eleven acres or more was sown as that make a lot of difference in the bulk. He said, "No," for the drill would only sow the amount if the right wheel were put on and that was done he knew. Yes, Revet, Bearded or Great Wheat. Some was grown at Borley many years ago - a lot of acres. This came to more than sixteen sacks [36 cwt.] per acre. Mr. J. L. Gardiner, the farmer's son, told me that the wheat stood as high as his father who was a tall man. He picked a lot of the wheat ears and counted the kernels - over eighty. He kept some of the ears for [many] years.

Wheat

---

[i] See below.
[ii] Presumably referring to the scent but perhaps not the 'nasty smell' mentioned on page 56.

Barley	I have mentioned two yields of wheat. I will of barley. But make no mistake Reader I speak of what I have heard. Also I warrant [that this] is also right if it could be proved. On Hill Farm, Gestingthorpe a field of barley came out at nineteen sacks [38 cwt.] per acre. A Mr. T. Taylor farmed this for many years. Several fields I have known came out at fifteen sacks [30 cwt.] per acre.
Oats	Of Oats - one Good Friday I went to Little Yeldham Hall for ten sacks [15 cwt.] of oats to sow on Osbourne's Field. We had to cut those oats by scythe and tie up, as they were down and twisted about. Those came to a lot over twenty sacks [30 cwt.] per acre. Sown with the same oats next year over ten sacks. I hired two and a half acres of this field, which was half of a five-acre field, a hedge being cut to part the field as it was added to the Auberies Estate. Some oats were sown for Mr. G. Badham who farmed the [original] five-acre Osbeans [or Osborns] Field. Mr. Badham died in the November of the year when these oats were sown [1877] - the Great Fire of Goldingham Hall was on October 6th. The oats, winter oats, came to a lot over fifty sacks. That was twenty sacks [30 cwt.] and more per acre. A friend of mine Mr.Frank Marsh, threshed a little field of oats for his uncle, Mr. Aubrey Chinnery, who died this year [1937] over eighty years old. These oats were from Gartons, a firm who specialised in Oats. There were over thirty sacks [45 cwt.] per acre. Mr. Frank Marsh was a partner of my brother [Albert] with one or two threshing sets of traction engine power.
Beans	A field of beans, five or six acres, was grown at Otten Belchamp by a Mr. J. Chatters, a cousin of my wife who had a small occupation with a little barn and a few outbuildings, but no house. This land was let to him by a Mr. Parmenter of Beverton Lodge or Hall - [which consisted of] two farms, one at the Hall and say another not far off, called Old House Farm. Those beans were threshed by flail by Mr. Chatters. He told me he took the beans in a horse and cart to Borley Mill. Mr. R. Payne had the mill and the large house and farms of Borley Hall and The Place. A very good farmer - one of the best. The beans came to twenty sacks [47.5 cwt.] per acre. [i] Many years ago beans grew in a little field called Pit Acre, a small field between the Old Lane and Gallows Green with Cross Path Ley on the north side. These beans were all put on one wagon and taken to the Hill Farm of Mr. Turner. There were twelve sacks of beans off that land when threshed by flail.

Instances of amazing tillers of wheat

At Bulmer Street	I will mention no more of corn yielding but will tell of a clump of wheat I saw grow in a garden under the eaves of a thatched house in Bulmer. One Sunday night when I came out of Bulmer Chapel, the old chap who lived there [Matthew Hall] asked me to count the ears of corn. When I was coming away from the wheat I had counted the ears thereof, a lady, Mrs. Burlingham of Griggs Farm, also came out of the chapel - my wife was her servant then, so it was before I was married. She asked me what Matthew Hall had asked me to look at. I told her his clump of wheat. "How many ears do you think there are on Mam?" I said. "Well there are seventy-two ears from one kernel of wheat that growed from the plant of wheat." "Well," the lady said, "we have read of sixty fold[ii] but that beat that."

---

[i] The editor is indebted to AC and *The Local Historian's Glossary of Words and Terms*, Bristow, 2001, for the conversion figures. See table on page 20.
[ii] Wheat usually has four to five tillers on a well-sown crop – AC.

Last year [1936] at Severall's I had a little garden in an empty fowl run. In the spring or early summer, in some grass that was growing I noticed a plant of wheat. So I cleared that grass from around it to give it a chance to grow well. This growed so fast and as the season came along [it] became a fine plant. I put sticks around so the wind would not beat it down as it grew. When the ears began to show in the green straws I put fine wire netting around to protect it from the sparrows. When all the wheat ears were out I counted them. There were sixty-six. These I showed to a friend who went around to have a chat and see around. I counted them so he could see how many for himself. He was surprised. [Apparently the sparrows did get in but after a considerable time the straw ripened and he adds] . . . for wheat or nearly all corn, the thicker it is the sooner the straw will ripen.

In Tulip's garden

Ten sacks of peas were sown on a field of ten acres. I went behind the drill. We had about enough peas. When the peas were cut some [men] used old scythes [and] some had a pea-make.[i] Some of the peas I pulled up to see the length of them. They were longer than I can reach. Those were threshed out of the field. Two days we were threshing them. The days were the 17th, 18th and 19th of September. It was so hot and dry they broke up into chaff. I was on the straw stack. Not a bad job, for it was hot and I did not make it big. It was so hot where the machine was standing - under the wind by a hedge where very little wind could get. Those on the machine put up an awning to keep the sun off. A thatcher I worked with for some years was thatching a big stack. He got overpowered by the sun or heat and fell off the ladder on the stack. He could do no more work that season. The field yielded ten sacks per acre. No extra, but when we cut those peas there was not a thistle above the peas, neither on the ground could one see a weed of any description unless there was a place the ground was bare. Surprising that, what land or what one seed can grow!

Peas

More of cutting, raking and stacking

I helped with two harvests at Goldingham Hall before my father lost his arm. The first was a half-man, a little more the next [year] and three-quarter–man the last time, after he lost his arm. If wheat were cut with scythe the two half-men tied up the wheat behind the Lord. That was the rule on that farm. Also they always had breakfast at nine o'clock - later there than anywhere I ever did harvest work. The reason was because the corn was often more fit to cart after ten o'clock. Also because if sixteen men were cutting wheat or barley, more was cut in a morning if carting commenced after breakfast. Readers must bear in mind that harvests were taken by the men at so much per acre all round that district. So the sooner the corn was cut and carted the more money was earned in the shortest time. The farmer had very little to do but tell the Lord his plans. So it could be haggled over by the leading men of the company. The money per week, £1 each per man, was given or lent to the Lord to distribute to his company.

Some organisational details

Workers' meal times

From the Sudbury Road to Goldingham Hall are two fields each a quarter of a mile long. I have heard my father and others say that three times the company of harvesters has cut down that field of wheat before breakfast at 9 o'clock. At that rate a man [will have] cut six feet - two yards at a swathe [as the swathes were

Exceptional quantities cut before breakfast

---

[i] A pea-make was a long-handled tool similar to a hedge-slasher, but with a finer scythe-type blade. See illustration, page 68.

two yards wide]. Five and a half yards is a rod, pole or perch. Eighty rods is an acre. A man could cut half an acre and more before breakfast and one man tied up half an acre. If there were sixteen men, as when I harvested there, those cut more than four acres, making a hole in the twenty-three acres of each of those two Church Fields [Upper and Lower] so named. One can see from end to end in both fields. In the Lower Church Field one can see the whole field at once as it is fairly level. [In this field, on] one Good Friday some years ago one or two barley stacks were threshed and the straw put on to [i.e. made into] one. There was a very high wind and the straw pitcher blowed over, the whole lot of straw being blown all over and about at the far end, so it had to be horse-raked up to clear the field.

Fields behind Bulmer Street

Trouble with strong winds

Carting sheaves and building stacks

Stack building

At a time I went to Goldingham Hall first, the wheat was cut with a reaping machine with four sails as before wrote of. When the wheat was carted there was no need for us two half-men. There were four men in the field when carting wheat and five men on the stack, but that depended on the size of the company. At one time there were four to four. When the stack was to be topped up a man was sent for out of the odd gang to help finish the stack so that wagons could be cleared as fast as they were loaded. If four men were on a big stack of sheaves then one man was on the load to un-pitch the sheaves, another was in the stage hole and two were left for topping up the roof of the stack. When a stack is made, a thick bottom of straw is laid down say six yards by twelve yards long. The first layer of sheave, or corn, is a little wider than the sticks put down to shape the bottom. When the stack is high and it is the height of the last layer before the middle is filled up, the men begin to put the roof on. Then it is too small for the two men to get rid of the sheaves fast. Also another bottom for the next stack is to be got, unless the farmer has men out of the harvest to do this work or he gives so much for the making of stack bottoms. On the farm I was, we had 10/- that was paid extra if the stack to be put-up next is some distance from the last stack. There are ladders, the men's baskets and bottles as well as clothes to be carried, for in harvest time if out in the fields one has to be prepared some days for a shower. Some farmers had big stack cloths to be put on the stacks at night. If not the men would have to cover the stack with some straw. Others do not. That is one reason why five men went to the stack at Goldingham Hall.

Raking fields

Raking

After a field was cleared of wheat, we two half-men had the job of horse raking. There was no seat on a horse-rake then. If we did ride it had to be on the rake behind and we did that if possible. But if the wheat was very strong laid - for if cut with a machine or reaper there were a lot of loose corn - there was little time to get on the rake to ride or we could not put the handle down to unload the rake. So we had to walk. Yes, and both of us walked over twenty acres in one day more than once.

Work with horses

Goldingham Hall was a good place for horses. There were plenty at the time we both were there. If no other was available we took a young horse that had only been broken in for a short time perhaps. I know I took one that had never been put in draughts before and that one was a black one, a beauty. It made the most money at the farm sale. A brewer bought it, but "that horse was too good," he told my father, for it was a wonder to get into a cart. It was a free horse. My father broke it in. He said he dare not hit it or move the plough cord to make it go, as some horses need. I put that in a horse-rake in a barley field, a long one at that, but with not too much to do to finish the field. That was the only horse left in the stable so I took it. I had to ride that horse and it went full trot until the field was done. I was glad for a change and I then had to go in a long field where wheat had been carted. Plenty to take up in long stubble. I had my fouress [*sic* - fowerses or beevers] before starting - a half-hour meal we used to stop for about five o'clock to half past and we needed it too sometimes when it was very hot. After the meal Poppet, that was the horse's name, thought she was going to keep up the trot. She thought better before she got to the quarter-mile. She was tamed by seven o'clock or a little after. One can easily knock up a horse on a horse-rake at that time of day, especially if one could ride on behind, which we did if possible. Then we boys got wrong [by] some of the men who said we did not do enough. But whether they meant what they said to us [or not] we did not like it and both of us would let out at them.

More of Workers' meals

Sometimes when carting, we of the odd gang [i.e. the half or three-quarter men] had to set up sheaves or tie up oats, or whatever there was to cut and tie before the barley was cut. No winter barley was grown anywhere near Bulmer. In fact I never saw winter barley till the Great War was on, when I thatched a stack of it in July - I think the last day or so of. It was more [often] near September before much barley was either cut or carted. But the seasons have changed a bit since. I know for I finished harvest very early September once when I was at Jenkins Farm after I got married [1896]. But when a half-man for two years or so and then a three-quarter-man we had a job to get finished before the sale [at Goldingham Hall] in early October [1888].

More of barley

No Winter barley

Barley was gathered different ways on different farms. But I never saw any done easier than that at the one I am writing of. These men always carted barley the same way as cut - up or down the swarths. Two of these [swarths] were gathered with forks - pitchforks if could be got. But there were forks on the market called shack forks; of two kinds - one with a short haft and totle [tote] or cross wood at the top for the hand, [the other] a long straight-shafted kind. Both were good for to put one swath on top of one the other side to that, making three in one. This I liked the best of all as each side of the wagon had the same size row for each forkful for the men to give the loaders on the wagon. There were usually two of these in big gangs. This was well also for us two half-men for we had three swaths each to rake. Also two men could gather with two pitchforks easily and then put the barley on straight. So it was good for picking up and also good for loading, for a not too big forkful could be picked well that would otherwise drop about.

Gathering barley

Putting two or three swaths together

At another farm where the company was about the same size they had all barley gathered with a hand rake. The worst tool on a farm for me to use. For to use a rake to put fairly heavy corn in heaps to cart, one had to grip the rake-haft tight. This would make my hands the sorest from any tool on a farm to be used. Hand rakes always try to make blisters on my hands and do if one cannot keep them level. These hand hafts are made of green wood of the right size, steamed and

Gathering barley with rakes

Hand rakes and blisters!

pressed, or set, to keep them straight - some do [so], but plenty do not. Also many of these are rough - not smooth until worn with thick hard gloves.

But gloves are not needed in hot weather unless there are a lot of thistles, as sometimes there are in barley, wheat and oats. Yes, if the sun is hot when tying wheat or loading barley without gloves the dear little sharp points of a thistle will keep one from going to sleep. Especially if a good one get under his finger nails - very sore they make a finger. I knew a man who was tying wheat or loading barley with a new pair of gloves. In a day or two after all his fingernails were turned black. They all came off after a time so he had a new set. I told him he ought to be thankful to have new for old. "Yes," he said, "but my old ones were very sore at the time." I will bet they were. His name was Shelley. A name not heard of in the parish now though a lot went to school. But there are a few descendants, not all of that name.

Gloves and thistles!

Cutting beans

Beans were sometimes cut very green on that farm and cut a few days before any harvesting was done at all. These would be cut around [the field perimeter] by some of the men on day work. Not so much was given for peas and beans - 10/- per acre or 1/- less sometimes if the corn etc was 12/- or a little more. So much was taken off for the reaper machine for wheat and oats - I think 2/6 per acre. One place I harvested was 3/- with the reaper, but that reaper carried the corn round the corners and that was not kicked or trodden about. These beans were tied up in the mornings if there was a very heavy dew or if it rained not too hard. Beans were good to have in a harvest as they keep men together. For in wet weather it please some, if they have any loose money in their pockets, for a rain, so then they could have a pint or two in the pub, for I would go and have a pint to 'clear the air' as it was called.

On some farms all beans were cut with a rip,[i] a sharp tool that is used to cut around fields, grass, brambles, wood etc. Beans were planted from twenty inches to two feet between the rows. One man cut four [rows]. The Lord [the] first four and the rest followed on. If a man did not turn up and he had not sent word to the Lord [that] he was ill, his four rows were left for him to do as best he could. At the next farm to this, Smeetham Hall, [there] was a large field [and] a little ditch was a part way down the field [with on one side a] piece of twenty-eight acres or more and [on] the other part eighteen acres [Great Broadfield]. So altogether it was a large field. The large piece afore mentioned was sown with clover in the barley. The clover did not plant [grow]. This was plowed up and sown with spring beans. All these were cut by hand - a lot of acres for any gang of harvesters. The beans grew late and kept on growing. Then they were all cut and [they] stood in the field a long time to get dry. They did not die till cut, but were carted when perhaps they were as well as they could be. I believe the beans were in the field when the farm sale was on for the Byfords, but I am not sure of this.

Threshing beans

I helped to thresh one of the bean stacks that came off that field. Those bean sheaves were as flat as boards. Looked as if they had been hot. For the beans were so green that few of the leaves had fallen off before they were cut. Yes, some of those sheaves were six feet long - plenty were five feet. I never seen beans so long since. That was in the year 1888; the last year the Byfords farmed the Hall I have been writing of till now [Goldingham Hall]. The springtime 1889 was when I

---

[i] See note iii page 46.

62

helped to thresh those beans at Smeetham Hall, Bulmer. Col. Burke was the owner - Mr. Godden, his bailiff. I know my uncle Charles and his son helped in the harvest at Smeetham Hall at the time.

One wet day, as soon as it left off raining some of the men went to cut the beans. The Lord, Mr. G. Felton, he was sure to go, for he was a good Lord for both master and man. A lot of men were not married of course. After the day got up they would call in at the Blackbirds, the nearest pub. The field could be seen well from the yard at the back. They would have a drink. Yes, and did not hurry over it. Soon, if it rained, a few more would come and say, "we will see how it is after dinner." Of course if it cleared up a bit some would [be] sure to go to cut the beans, for the drops of rain are soon gone by a little breeze from anything, which is wet, [both] off the ground and in the open. Yes, then they would work as hard as they could to get their four rows cut as fast as they could, whether behind or in front. Some days if as that mentioned, several others came in from the farms where they harvested; nothing was doing for they had no cutting to do. All they could do is perhaps turn barley. This is not done in the afternoons. Such like is done as soon as it is a bit dry on the top and there is not too much to do. Some farmers did not have their barley turned, for when barley is cut first it lies on a ridge of stubble, so the barley ears are not on the ground. When the weather is warm, barley will soon sprout - not so quick if cold.

Wet weather days

Carting when damp

The Mr. D. Gardiner was the most particular man one could work for with corn, for he did not like to cart wheat if a heavy dew. I know if there was a wet barleycorn in a field he would find it and he did not like carting barley if it was ever so slightly damp in the morning, but he said nothing of it at night. I know I asked him once why he was so particular, for other folk were carting - "so and so do but you do not," [I said]. He was good, he did not mind anyone asking him of anything at times - most of us knew when we could. "Well," he said, "Philip, I like my corn got up so I can have any stack threshed when I like. Unlike those who cart the corn when they do. Also corn got up in good condition is better for cattle and wheat that is got up well is much better for us people to eat." And I can say in the ten years I harvested for him he had only one barley stack got warm and that was stacked near the Old Barn near where I lived. He walked up to that stack a few days before he was satisfied with it, to be sure it did not get too hot. I told him it would not, but it got warm in and near the stage hole, being where nearly all the barley were unloaded. The chaff, or avels, fell all over the barley with the little clover that he did not like to cart so quick [soon] - for there was some in that field that was not too fit. That was the reason it got a little warm.

Yet during the time The Great War was on I thatched - not on Mr. Gardiner's farm, even if he was still there - wheat stacks that after I had thatched, the one could see the steam coming through the thatch on top of the stack. As much as one could expect off a hay stack. These are best if they are a bit warm or hot if the hay is carted without rain. If it does [rain] this water heats and the hay gets mouldy for a lot of the stack. Not so if it is the sap of hay or clover. Hay is much better to get hot, but not too hot. For I have trussed hay - also clover - that in the middle of the stack it has been black. One can rub it up as if charred by fire. Such

Hot stacks

stacks are so hot as near being fired as anything. If cut at the time and left open to wind it would burn.

The Lord of the Harvest, Largesse and the Harvest Supper

I have written of my experiences of being Lord of the Harvest, of which my father and grandfather was one, also my uncle [Charles] and one of his sons, as well as some relations on my mother's side. My father used to book and helped me some years ago do the counting up, as it wants a bit of doing with a lot of acres at different prices. As this was with him, so with me. Not a very thankful office to be a lord, especially along with some men. Men who had been used to the master to order them do not like to be ordered by one of their own class. Funny to think there should be a difference. But if a master advertise for a foreman [from elsewhere] he is made more of than one of their fellow mates. But I always could take an order off a mate as well as a master be he who he would be. Very often masters are not fair to their man who is Lord at harvest time. I know my father was not behaved well to. A Lord is picked out by harvestmen very often. Why? Because the men know he know how to do the work and how it should be done. Also he does not flinch at what he says before a master. He is not afraid to ask the master for more money if the work is worth more, as it is in some years. For in a year that the corn is knocked about and twisted by the rough weather, he is not afraid to tell the master they ought to have more per acre. I have cut barley when the best way is to cut a stetch at a time. Two men on a stetch so the men are not in each others way and they can get at the laid corn as best they can. Also others know what they have to do, for if the Lord and his Lady take a stetch to do, the others will have to be busy.

A harvest dispute

I was going to mention the following incident. I went to school at the time.[i] I am going to blame no one in particular, for the husband of the lady who my father worked for was dead - her eldest son paid out the money. They had a working foreman. A man with a large family. He did the thatching - his son helping him. A very good sort of man, but one who when they come into a fresh parish with their master, seems to think and talk as if no one could do work like them and those where they came from. There were also executors who came once or twice a week to superintend the farm. One was a decent sort of man who was uncle to the family.

The men were to go to the farm before they left off to try and take the harvest.[ii] A shilling per man was given to bind him. In some places glove-money was given. Beer was no doubt taken from the house, for these Byfords were very good at beer. However they did not take it the first night. They were not offered enough money. They left it and had to go another time, a night or two after. It was the same. They held out. My father had a nephew [George] who was a plowman working with him - a good man with horses who had won prizes for plowing. He was some bit over twenty years old. I expect they said as much as any, for they were both good scholars and not afraid to speak before a master - not behind his back. Although those kind were made to suffer if they liked their homes and also the part around them where they and their neighbours lived, [for] both men knew that those cottages where they lived and were brought up belonged to the farm

Problems with tied houses

[i] Probably not. See note ii on page 65 & note i, page 66.
[ii] Negotiate the terms and settle the deal.

64

[and] they would have to find another place to live whether they wanted to or not. The house would have been wanted for another man. Often such was the case.

As they did not take the harvest that night it was left over for the executor to let it. But my father and cousin both had the sack. Poor old chap I call him, but he was not old then. I know he had planned to brew for the harvest the next day so he did not go to see about another harvest, for brewing is a busy day. He had got his malt and hops but could not brew as his turn had not come for the use of the copper and tubs etc. Perhaps the neighbours had their malt etc come before or father's casks were not quite empty, either way it had to be done before they got busy with the harvest.

I feel sure the men took the harvest that night, for when our neighbours came home from work one of them told father they had taken the harvest and he could go back and do his usual work or job. This man who had worked on the farm for many years was a day man - a good one too. There was no work on a farm other than horse work he could not do. A good mate, not afraid of his master. A real old Liberal and a Union one at that - if the Union was in go [at that time].[i] When he got to the bake house where father was brewing he told father that the old man was there, the executor. They took the harvest at their price; nothing was said to the contrary. "I did not say anything," he said, "I thought I would listen. The fools. Just before we took the shilling I said to the old man, "Sir, it is not fair to settle without those two who have had the sack for speaking up." Says the old chap, "I did not know." No names. My father had left [but] he could come back. Nothing was said of my cousin although there were several young single men there. Humbugs. I know I should have done so if I thought myself a man. He brought a shilling for my father. I was listening and looking. I saw the moisture in my father's eye. "Aye, Fred boy, I had better go back, all harvests are let by now. But I wish some had spoken for George because he perhaps would not have said so much if it had not been for me. He ought to go back as well." Yes, good men both of them. My cousin did not get a harvest that year, but he got other work and did not have to loose much time. But he did not get so much money as he would have got at a harvest.

Tulip's cousin looses his job for speaking out

I believe that it had been thought out by the farmers all round, as on the Farm Jenkins there had been a stir up between some of the men and Mr. D. G. Gardiner, although I did not hear lot of it. Men do not as a rule talk a lot before boys, for no one knows how far a tale goes. I was always told not to go near men when [they were] talking unless I spoke so they saw me. Neither to repeat anything said that matters.

Men come from Cambridge

Anyway, on Jenkins Farm that year [c1886][ii] a gang of men came from Cambridge. They were fossil diggers of coprolite[iii] or some such name. This was

Men are hired from Cambridgeshire for general and harvest work on Bulmer farms

---

[i] Unions fluctuated at this time – AC.
[ii] Before 1882 if Tulip was still at school, but elsewhere he states he was fifteen. See note page 66.
[iii] Coprolite is fossilised dung unearthed and used as a fertilizer – over 40yrs later Tulip on one of his 'wanderings' was to see the remains of these workings which he describes as ' hills and holes' near Swaffham, Cambs.

made into fertilizers or manures. Nine men came with a lot of big casks with straw for to sleep on. These men came to do the harvest on Jenkins Farm. For why? I never did know, not to this day the reason. Mr. D. Gardiner got two men, father and son for harvest at Gentry Farm. Another man went to a brother-in-law at Street Farm, Great Henny. Four horsemen, or two horsemen and two others - day plowmen who used horses but did not feed them on Sundays - went with a tumbrel and two horses to a chalk pit and put as much chalk onto the cart as possible to put on the land. A good many acres were chalked on the farm that season. They had to go four or five times per day. The fields [looked] like as if snow had fell on them, for they looked so white. Of course a harvest day was from six o'clock in the morning to seven or half past at night, if carting to dusk. A nice lot of men. Of course the men of the parish did not think well of them to come and take the quickest money to be earned, if not the hardest. For often if a harvest took five weeks to get in at £ [*sic* – sum not specified] per week for five weeks, then when settled up £3 or more was a lot better wage than the ordinary wage of 10/- or 12/- per week. This extra would buy some new clothes or new shoes etc.[i]

The Largesse or Horkey

Collecting the Largeese

After harvest, different companies of harvestmen would have their largesse spending, for at that time the masters gave to the men in the harvest 1/- for binding money, 6d for largesse and 2/6 or 3/- per man hockey[ii] money. The first Saturday after the harvest was over the monies was eked out, often at The Cock or The Blackbirds - as it called by either name by local residents. The men would go off to the town and a few, with the Lord of the Harvest or foreman, would go to the tradesmen who supplied the master of the farm with any commodities and get a largesse off them. All the tradesmen would give a trifle. The thatcher, wheelwright, plough maker and machinery maker were called upon. If the shooting on the farm was let, as it were in some cases, the gentleman that bought the shoot gave a good one - £1 or more if lucky. If the masters had the shoot themselves they gave a little and when the sportsmen came for a day's partridge shooting some of the men would go to the sportsmen and touch them for largesse. They got in that way a good sum.

---

[i] In another narrative Tulip adds the following information concerning the men from Cambridgeshire. 'The men . . . came to do the harvest for something or other [for] the man I worked for. I tended sheep and was about fifteen years old. I never heard how it came about, but the men had some dispute with the master about carting some hay or clover. He discharged six men or more just on the harvest time. Three or four [of the men] got a harvest on another farm, [but they] had to come back to him [the Master] at the finish. There were nine of them and good men too – knew how to harvest and drink beer too. Good company. It was said at the time it was a planned job with the Farmers Union. Be it as it may, or whose fault it was [I know not]. They did the work no better than those men belonging to the parish. I know it would not have done if his own men had sent loads home without being raked down, for there was a great lot of barley strawn [*sic*] along the cart-way; more than would had his own men did the harvesting. I had a sheepdog to help me with the sheep – a rare dog to hunt. If it saw a rabbit or hare I could not keep him from running after it. I know these men used him at night and early morning for sometimes he was nearly knocked up. One day he went and laid up at my home. The master would not have liked that.'

[ii] 'Hockey' and 'horkey' are both used for the harvest home supper – see *The Suffolk Dialect of the 20th Century*, Claxton, 1960 - note Tulip's distinction below, between 'harvest supper' and 'harvest home'.

The Horkey

The hockey or harvest supper was on a Saturday afternoon and night - two feeds. All the men of the farm with their wives had a good dinner of beef and mutton, boiled and baked. My father being Lord of the Harvest found the potatoes for the feast. He was paid for the potatoes when the harvest was squared up on the Monday night. Some stayed for supper. All having a good time with plenty of ale, plenty of music and dancing and some good old English songs and recitations that a few were very good at. Several would play an accordion or concertina or a chance one a fiddle or a violin. On the Monday night the men and lads only cleared up the remains, settled for the ale and cooking and paid up the amount that was required, all wishing one and another well and hoping to have another next year. Very little was to pay for this supper between the company and the men who took part, for all those who worked on the estate were entitled to go to the supper. One place I harvested at the families were all provided for, even if schoolchildren or the boys worked on other farms. Good times, good mates, but very little more outings till another harvest was come and finished off in this way. Some companies had their children with them at the same occasions if they could not be left with a neighbour or relative, but 'twas not so at The Cock. Neither ought it to be so for with ale and by having too much, things were said that ought not to be said. These suppers were enjoyed by all who attended them, but a harvest supper is seldom heard of now [1937].

The 'Harvest Home'

Two or three parishes had a harvest home, where all the parish were invited. This was a grand affair, although I cannot tell of it but hearsay of some lads of my age who had been to Great Henny, Belchamp Walter and Foxearth - Foxearth being the last I think held near Bulmer. Of course these things are of the past. My father, uncle and others said, "a good thing too." Although they joined in and enjoyed the fun, they said it was all very well for the masters and clergy and ladies and gentlemen to give something to the poor to have sports and a good feed and the like, but why not order it so the farm workers had more money every week so they could get some good food for themselves – with a little bit of meat during the week.

Tulip's postscript

Here I will say that harvesting is [now, 1937] quite different in all ways to then. If better or worse I do not know for I have only helped in one harvest since the war began in 1914. The next year I did thatching with two of my sons and since then till the last time always with two of my sons. The last harvest only one son came thatching. I did not have so many farms or there was not so much corn grown as the acreage fell off for a year or two before. The last harvest I was at home, I harvested for my brother Albert. I and my brother Sid or one of my sons helping me thatch his stacks. This was in 1923, so I have only helped in one harvest since 1914. So one may not wonder at me not knowing anything about the difference there is in harvesting and the time I have been writing of. Well I do [know this] for then it were let by acre [at] so much to cut and cart; now harvesting is either a bounty for, or so much per hour.

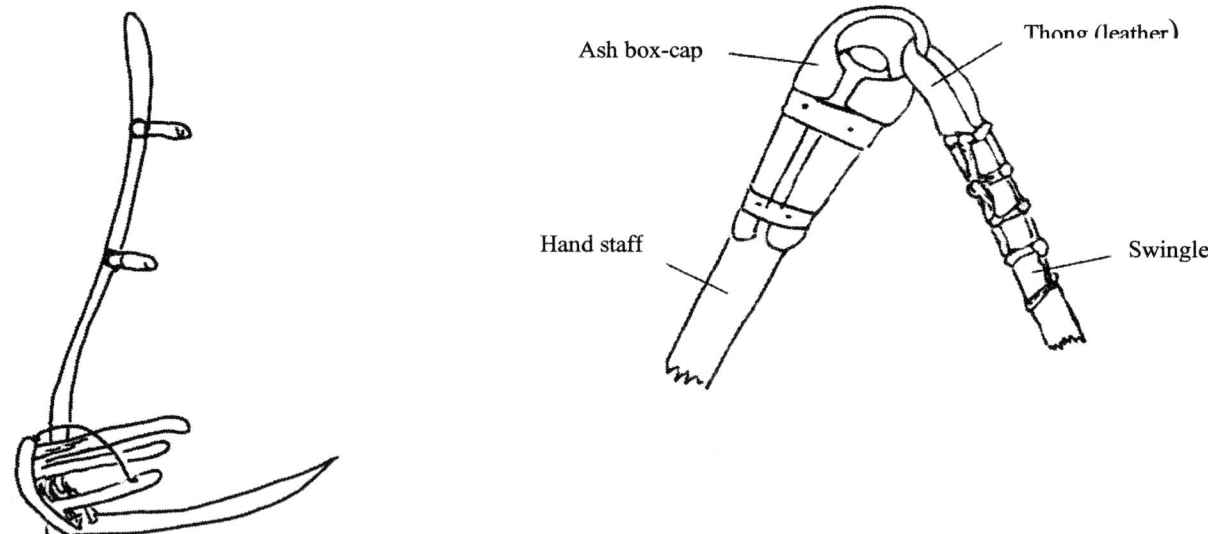

Fig 7: Scythe with cradle

Fig 8: Flail Joint – sketched from an Essex example –
probably of the type known to Tulip

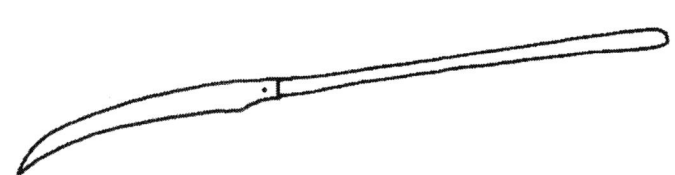

Fig 9: A Pea-make

1: Hilda	14: Stanley	27: **Emily Cornell (née Rowe)**
2: Rose (née Weavers)	15: Arthur Raymond (33, 32, 34)	28: <u>**David**</u>
3: Bernard	16: **Charles (Charlie)** (36, 37, 35)	29: <u>**Eliza**</u>
4: **Harry** (2, 19, 14, 1, 3, 18)	17: **George** (38)	30: **Phillip (Tulip)** (31, 9, 13,
5: **Albert** (21, 20)	18: Sidney (Young Sid)	11, 12)
6: Gertrude (Gertie)	19: Elsie	31: Mary (née Martin)
7: **James (Jim)** (23, 22)	20: Maud (Maudie)	32: Robert Raymond (Bob)
8: **Sidney (Sid)** (24, 6, 25)	21: Laura (Lolly, née Humm)	33: **Agnes (née Rowe) (Aggie)**
9: **Frederick* (Fred)**	22: Phyllis	34: Eva Raymond
10: John Cornell (27, 26)	23: Amy (née Briggs)	35: Mabel
11: **Thomas* (Tom)**	24: Annie (née Turps)	36: Mabel (née Pearce)
12: **William* (Billie)**	25: Edith (Eadie)	37: Florence (Jenny)
13: **Phillip* (Phil)**	26: John Cornell	38: Ethel

N.B: David & Eliza (bold, underlined), their children (bold), Tulip's sons (bold*) All married males have their spouse and children - by age – in brackets after their name.

Key to figures in Rowe family picture – Fig 10 (opposite)

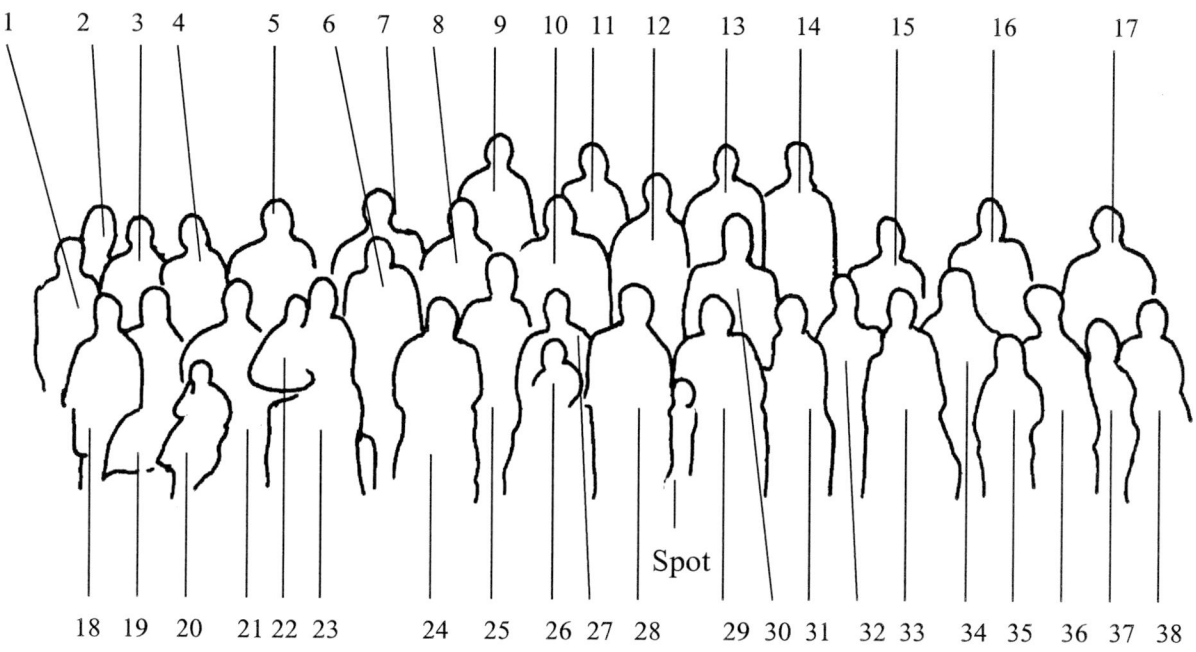

Fig 10: David and Eliza Rowe with their family 1919

APPENDIX I

DETAILS OF ORIGINALS:

Lined Exercise Books. (Dimensions in inches)

Book I	6 ¼" X 4"	October 1st – October 10th 1927	90 Pages	S
Book II	"	November 24th – December 3rd 1927	116 Pages	S
Book III	"	December 10th 1927	85 Pages	S
Book IV	"	December 23rd – December 26th 1927	98 Pages	S
Book V	"	December 29th 1927 – January 7th 1928	102 Pages	S
Book VI	"	January 7th – January 16 1928	84 Pages	S
Book VII	"	January 19th – January 27th 1928	88 Pages	S
Book VIII	"	February 21st – February 25th 1928	114 Pages	S
Book IX	"	February 25th – March 4th 1928	104 Pages	S
Book X	"	March 4th – March 12th 1928	113 Pages	S
Book 11a	8 ¼" X 6 ½"	October 29th 1936	25 Pages	H
Book 11b	"	December 13th 1936	34 Pages	H
Book 11c	"	February 18th 1937	34 Pages	S
Book 12	"	February 24th 1937	24 Pages	S
Book 13	"	undated	28 Pages	S
Book 14	"	February 28th 1937	12 Pages	S
Book 15	"	March 1st 1937	88 Pages	S
Book 16	12 ¾" X 8"	March 9th 1937	184 Pages	S
Book 17	8 ¼" X 6 ½"	May 1st 1938	39 Pages	H *

S = Written at Severall's Hospital

H = Written at Home (Upper Houses, Bulmer)

* Some of this written as a diary during a journey.

INDEX
Heavy type refers to maps and illustrations.

ISBN 0-9548936-0-3

Price: £5.50